MUCH ABOUT KILMACOLM

A FAMOUS OLD HEALTH-GIVING
PART OF SCOTLAND.

CONTAINING ALSO

A PLEASING ACCOUNT OF THE COUNTRY AND
VARIOUS PLACES ROUND THE VILLAGE.

BY

ALEXANDER S. GIBB,

AUTHOR OF "TRANSLATIONS FROM BUCHANAN'S JEPTHA AND BAPTIST," ETC.

> "Here be woods as green
> As any; air likewise as fresh and sweet
> As where smooth Zephyrus plays on the fleet
> Face of the curled stream, with flowers as many
> As the young spring gives, and as choice as any
> Here be all new delights, cool streams and wells,
> Arbours o'ergrown with woodbines, caves and dells:
> Choose where thou wilt, whilst I sit by and sing,
> Or gather rushes to make many a ring
> For thy long fingers."

FLETCHER's *Faithful Shepherdess.*

WITH A NEW ESSAY ON
HABBIE SIMPSON & KILBARCHAN

BY

CHRIS MORRISON & NORMA J. LIVO

THIS EDITION
THE GRIAN PRESS
2004

First published 1872

This edition 2004
Some revisions made July 2004
Published by The Grian Press
7 New Street
Paisley PA1 1XU
Scotland UK

ISBN: 0954799607

CONTENTS.

	PAGE
PREFACE,- -	v
ARRIVAL AT KILMALCOLM, - - - - - - - - - - - - -	1
KILMALCOLM, -	2
SHORT WALKS AND RAMBLES	
ROUND THE VILLAGE, - - - - - - - - - - - - - -	10
KILMALCOLM - ECCLESIASTIC, - - - - - - - - - -	15
CHURCHES IN KILMALCOLM, - - - - - - - - - - -	24
KILMALCOLM AS A PLACE OF RESIDENCE,	
AND FOR SUMMER VISITORS, - - - - - - - - - -	26
A DAY AMANG THE HEATHER, - - - - - - - - - - -	31
A VISIT TO DUCHAL CASTLE,- - - - - - - - - - - -	35
A VISIT TO FINLAYSTON GLEN AND HOUSE, - - -	41
ALEXANDER, THE FIFTH EARL OF GLENCAIRN,	
CALLED THE "GOOD EARL," THE FRIEND,	
OF KNOX, -	49
POEM ON THE GRAY FRIARS, - - - - - - - - - - - -	52
JAMES, THE FOURTEENTH EARL,	
THE PATRON OF BURNS,- - - - - - - - - - - - - -	61
FINLAYSTONE COUNTRY ESTATE, - - - - - - - - -	66
A VISIT TO BADRENEY, THE BOGLE STANE,	
NEWARK CASTLE, PORT-GLASGOW,	
AND DEVOL'S GLEN, - - - - - - - - - - - - - - - -	68
THE VISION OF AULD DUNROD, AT THE BOGLE	
STANE, -	83
VISIT TO BRIDGE OF WEIR AND,	
KILBARCHAN, - - - - - - - - - - - - - - - - - - -	89
ELEGY ON HABBIE SIMPSON I, - - - - - - - - - - -	93
NEW ESSAY ON HABBIE SIMPSON, - - - - - - - - -	97
ALEXANDER SCOTT'S POEM "of may," - - - - - -	103
ELEGY ON HABBIE SIMPSON II,- - - - - - - - - - -	109
A STORY OF GREENOCK, - - - - - - - - - - - - - -	121

PREFACE.

THIS edition of Alexander Gibb's charming work on Kilmacolm & environs introduces THE GRIAN PRESS. With his spirited and care-free observations on the lore and old-ways of
Kilmacolm and Renfrewshire, garnished with verses and
quaint quotes, it seemed an appropriate place to slot in our
essay on Habbie Simpson & Kilbarchan.

As was the way in 1872 the author refers to *Kilmacolm* as
Kilmalcolm, commenting upon the earliest form of the word
being *Kylmalcolm,* as written in the Chartulary of Paisley.
We have followed the original spelling throughout the text
except for the cover, title page and headers.

There is no need to explain the familiar image on the front
cover to those many ramblers and cyclists who like to savour
the peace of the car-free track amidst the verdure of the
Renfrewshire countryside.

Enjoy!

Chris Morrison.

THE GRIAN PRESS,
PAISLEY, July 2004.

MUCH ABOUT KILMALCOLM.

WE are speeding along on the railway from Paisley to Greenock. We have just stopped at Bridge-of-Weir, a thriving and growing manufacturing place. and are now crossing the Gryfe, here a stream of some size, and are soon sweeping up the valley of Kilmalcolm, on our way to that village. Past low hills, where wave woods dark with foliage, past farm houses and green fields, woods, moors, and marshes, the train speeds on, and gives us small time indeed for observation; for of all modes of locomotion that of a railway train is the worst for beholding the beauties of the landscape. Soon we are rattling through a deep cutting in hard whin rock; the whistle sounds, and the train comes to a stop at Kilmalcolm railway station, and we soon find ourselves on the platform. Thereafter, gentle reader, we established ourselves amid comfortable surroundings for a space of some weeks, and, having set ourselves to learn what is most notable in the neighbourhood, we will now proceed to put it before you, craving, therefor, your fair and generous consideration.

*　　　*　　　*　　　*　　　*

KILMALCOLM.

OF the position of the village, we remark that it lies in a corner of the valley, and is sheltered from the northerly and easterly blasts by a low range of braes called the Barclaven hills, which break out in some places into low crags. Till a few years ago, when the railway went through, it was little known, owing to its secluded situation; but, since railway communication has been established with Greenock, Paisley, and Glasgow, its excellence as a place of residence, and for summer visitors in quest of health and strength, has been rapidly becoming better known; and, judging from present appearances, it bids fair soon to rival the villa-towns of the coast. As we look around, we descry many tasteful new villas already built, and others in course of rapid erection. Several neat cottages also, with smiling gardens, and various handsome new shops, give a suburban air to the place. As we cast our eyes around, we see no furnace nor tall chimney belching forth its volumes of black smoke to darken the sky and pollute the air. This of itself should recommend the place to all to whom the restoration of health is a primary end in leaving the smoky city. Nor, while the weal of the body is likely to be furthered by an abiding at Kilmalcolm, is provision wanting for religious observance. Here is a neat U.P. Church and Manse, which were built in the years 1861-2. Opposite is the Parish School. Let us now proceed to the Parish Church, which, with its spire, forms a commanding object in all views of the village. The present church was built in the years 1833-34 for the late minister, Mr. Cameron. On the east of the present church stands the burial vault of the Porterfields of Duchal. The following inscription is cut out on a slab:-

> "Byreit heir lyis
> That deth defyis
> Of Porterfeilds the race,
> Quho be the spirit
> To Christ united
> Are heirs of glor through grace."

And beneath is the date 1560, the earliest record of this family in the parish. Inside is an anagram of a curious nature, which is worth puzzling over in some half-hour of leisure:-

> "This anagram unfold--my buildar sall
> His name quha vil into this sentence seik
> Till flie the it make guid report of al
> Guilliame sal find Porterfield of that ilk.
> Zeirs sevintie five to live he livit and mo
> But nov for ay livs vith ye Gods but vo."

At the east end of the church is the burial vault of the family of Glencairn. Of their right of sepulchre here the family were so jealous that, when they left the parish, on the estate devolving on R. Graham, Esq. of Gartmore, in 1796, in the deeds connected with the patronage they are careful to retain the right of sepulchre, although otherwise the patron would, from his possession of the patronage, have likewise a right of burial. One of the burial places of the Earls of Glencairn is Kilmaurs, in Ayrshire, where is a monument raised to them. One of them, William, ninth Earl, Lord Justice General of Scotland, who died in 1664, from chagrin at Archbishop Sharp obtaining precedence over him, was buried in St. Giles Cathedral in Edinburgh. Earl James, the patron of Burns, was buried at Falmouth, where he died, and Earl John, his brother, the last Earl, who died in the year 1796, was buried in St. Cuthbert's Churchyard in Edinburgh, where is a monument raised to his memory. In the old church, which was taken down in 1833 to make way for the new one, this vault was placed within the church at the end directly under the loft or gallery that was set aside for the Earl, his family, and attendants. There were two finely carved chairs for the great folk, and an earl's coronet overhead. It gives us a pleasing picture of auld warld times to think of the potent earls worshipping with their lowly countrymen, and the latter unenvious of the marks of superior dignity which should fitly attend superior rank. The gallery projected a little over what is now the vault, and on this seat, under his lordship's ken, and full in the sight of the minister, was the seat for delinquents who were to be rebuked for gross and open sins. The men in fault stepped in at one door and slunk out at the other. It happened once, however, when the terrors of the pulpit were beginning to be shorn of their power, that Wally M'Gown, game-keeper to the Earl of Glencairn, was to be rebuked in the face of the congregation for an affair with a young woman of the parish. He came in, and sat down in the seat, but so contrived it that two of his dogs got in along with him. When the minister called out in a loud voice, "Stand up, sir," Wat jumped to his feet and showed, first his face covered with the back of his wig (for he wore a wig), then, wheeling suddenly round, he presented the back of his head adorned with the same appendage. As the minister was becoming nettled at such contumacious behaviour, and began rating him in a loud key, M'Gown fetched a tremendous kick at the two sleeping brutes, who set up such a frightful barking and howling that not a word of the minister's address was heard, the congregation became confused, and in the midst of the hubbub that followed Wat slipped out at the door and went on his way. The law of fines for disturbing public worship had not, it seems, been in existence in those times, else our hero might have found himself soused in £50 of a fine. When John Knox, in 1556, visited Finlayston Castle, and dispensed the Sacrament to the Earl, his lady, two of his sons, and a few friends, there were no cups of the proper kind for holding the Sacramental wine, and in the emergency the hollow soles of two candlesticks of the finest silver were used instead. These screwed into the upper part. These interesting relics were always lent by the noble family of Glencairn to be used at the Sacraments in the Parish Church, and were much esteemed by the folk on account of their antiquity and history. On the family leaving the parish at the end of last century, the Countess of Glencairn took them with her, and supplied others to the parish instead. We have heard it said that they came to the hammer about five years ago in Edinburgh. Pity were it should they be lost.

We shall now take a turn through the old parts of the village; and, inasmuch as in a few years, in every likelihood, the rude and old-fashioned dwellings will be taken down, we shall give a more exact and full description of them. It has been long and far famed for being a queer place, queerer

even than the 'Shaws, and we may safely say that it is as
queer and droll-looking a hamlet as any in broad Scotland.
The walls of the old houses are built of unhewn stone, are
by no means plumb in many cases, and sometimes a block
which would not rightly fit into the wall is left jutting out.
The roofs are thatched, and the chimneys have been
compared to beehives stuck on the roofs. The houses have
been set down at all angles to the street, every builder
having, as it seems, followed the bent of his own whimsey.
Kailyards and houses are mixed up together. The office of
Her Majesty's mails is a low thatched house, such as we
have described. Of the interior arrangements we need not
speak: some houses have the large, old-fashioned, wide
chimneys still found in out-of-the-way country places; in
others the fire-place is, as it were, set to the wall, instead of
being sunk into it. None, however, have the arrangement
which old folks still remember to have been common in
farm-houses and cot-houses about the end of last century. In
that case the peat fire was put in a hole in the middle of the
floor, and a crook was suspended above from the roof. The
inmates sat on forms set around the fire. Right above was a
hole in the roof, at which, as well as at doors and windows,
the reek of the peats was expected to make its escape. On
either side were apertures termed "levers," by opening and
shutting of which, according to the point from which the
wind was blowing, the fire could be made to burn more
briskly, and the reek urged on its outward way. Peats were
flung up ready for use on a sort of wooden loft that ran
along the inside of the roof., The first change on that
system, which is still in use in some parts of the Highlands,
and likely differs little from the custom of the Gael in their

huts, when they first left Gallia for Albion, was to fill up the hole, and substitute an iron framework, which stood on the floor. No specimen of either of these ways now exist in the parish. But, to return to the village. Here, over the door of a public-house, we observe St. Malcolm, the patron saint of the village, a noble-looking and venerable old gentleman, with a crook in his hand, and a fine flowing beard. Here is the market place, a quadrangular space sixty yards square, where of old time fairs were wont to be held, and folks from the neighbouring parishes did congregate to do business. On a stone above the lintel of a door we see the date 1636, but this stone, we are told, was taken from a neighbouring farm belonging to one of the Hamilton family, whose initials, J. H., is also cut out on it. These old-fashioned dwellings seem to have undergone little change for centuries. In old times queer folks, such as are found in most villages, were found here too-rural philosophers, who denied the motion and rotundity of the earth. One old man thought that the world was coming to an end when he first saw loaf bread brought into the house. Another declared that, "as lang as the Misty Law stood on the ither side o' the water, naebody wad persuade him that the warl' was either roun' or gaed roun'." But the visitor will enquire in vain for such now. Formerly weaving was the chief trade of the place: the click of the shuttle was to be heard in every house. The webs were muslin, and were woven for the Paisley houses. A carrier went weekly to Paisley for the webs. One informant told us he remembered when there were thirty weavers in Kilmalcolm: now there is not one. One knight of the shuttle was wont very judiciously to take a day every week to himself for fishing in the Clyde. There were also several wheelwrights and clockwrights. One of these, James Park, was employed by many noble ladies to make spinning-wheels for them, to employ their vacant hours. He also invented the self-acting watershed for lobby doors, and was altogether a very ingenious person. Here also lived Johnnie Robinson, a shoemaker, who knew all the auld warld lore of the village and parish, and nothing gave him greater delight than to share it with a stranger. Of old most of the families were connected by kindred. This couplet gives the chief names of the inhabitants of old:-

> "Lang, Laird, Blair, and Holm,
> The chief names in Kilmalcolm."

We may say, in fine, that many of the inhabitants are striving to keep up with the times, and that better and better-looking houses are taking the places of the old-fashioned domiciles. The population of the village, by the census of 1871, was 395, and that of the parish 1765. Old customs also are still in vogue in the country parts of the parish, such as "rockings," or gatherings of young folk to spend an evening at singing a sang-about, with now and then the interlude of a dance. The "rocking" derives its name from the time when "the rock and the wee pickle tow" formed the usual employment of households in the evening. Now, of course, that part of the evening's labour is disused. "Riding the braise," or "brewis," is also sometimes practised here, as it is very commonly in the upper ward of Lanarkshire, and in other places. When the wedding party are drawing near the future home of the young couple, some of the best-mounted young men set off and ride a race. Whoever first reached the house is supposed originally to have been regaled with the "brewis" preparing for the wedding dinner, and therefore the custom was called "riding for the brewis." Now-a-days, however, a bottle of whiskey, wine, or ginger-cordial is substituted, and with this the successful youth returns to the party, when the bride and bridegroom drink to his good health. The "brewis" is sometimes run instead of ridden, and is altogether a very happy break in the dullness of wedding parties.

*   *   *   *   *

SHORT WALKS AND RAMBLES ROUND
THE VILLAGE

As we leave the snug village we hear the sparrows chirping on the roofs. We cross the railway, and remark the long cutting through the hard whin rock, which lies at a very short distance below the soil. The whin is the common rock of the parish, and, as is well known, affords a good soil for cereals and grasses. It crumbles into a dry and friable mass, which allows rain-water rapidly to sink into it, and be carried away. Were the soil clay, on the other hand, with a moist climate such as Kilmalcolm has in common with all the West of Scotland, the climate would be much colder, and less healthy. We pass the entrance to Duchal House, and a row of villas, erected or erecting, on our right. A little further on we reach the Mill, and cross the Gryfe, here a small, dark stream, fringed with a few stunted alder bushes. The tenantry on the baronies in old times were all sucken, or thirled to grind their corn at the baron's mill. This would be needful in old times, when none but barons and men of like rank would have means to erect a mill, or, likely enough, intelligence to make use of it. But such a state of things does not now exist in the whole of Scotland. As we go along we admire the daisies dappling the fields--

"Wee modest crimson-tipped flower,"

as it is so felicitously described by our great bard. We hear the lark carolling high in the sky with ringing cheerful notes. Turning up at the Bridgend Toll, we climb the brae a little way, solacing our thirst at a fine well, wherein a speckled trout is disporting himself. Many a pleasant well does every roadside here present, to refresh the wayfarer in the summer. Here we rest awhile to admire the village, for this is the point from which the best view of it is to be obtained. And very snug and sweet it looks, nestling in a corner of the hills, which shelter it so snugly. The Parish Church forms a conspicuous object in the centre, and new snowy-white villas rising around impart to it an air of elegance and richness. The odd-looking old tumble-down buildings are not seen at our point of view.

Our next walk begins somewhat unpromisingly, for we pass through a farm court-yard, and then ascend the brae past the old farm-house of High Shields, now rapidly falling to ruin, and doomed, in all probability, to be swept away in the enthusiasm for building and for improvements of every kind. Here is a very good well springing off the hard rock. An ancient villager was wont to go hither every morning, summer and winter, for his morning draught, deeming that there was a blessing in it. As we rise higher, we stop, turn round, and survey the scene below. The hollow plain we see beneath us is the Vale of Kilmalcolm, the highest part of the Valley of Strathgryfe--not very high, however, for the village is only about 350 feet above the level of the sea. It is of a uniform feature, and shelves down on both sides towards the Gryfe. The soil, which lies on hard whinstone, cropping out here and there in bare rocks, is well fitted both for cereals and for pasture, especially for the latter, which may account for the excellence of the milk, butter, and cheese of the dairies, which supply the wants of Greenock and Port-Glasgow. These lands were in early times divided into the two baronies, Duchal and Danielstoun, or Denni-estoun. The latter stretched from the Gryfe to the Clyde, and was latterly divided into Finlayston and Newark. The barony derived its name from a noble of the name of Daniel, of whom nothing is known. It bore the name as early as the reign of Malcolm IV. Sir Hugh de Danielston, of the county of Renfrew, did homage to Edward I., in 1296. Sir John Danielston was lord of Danielston in 1367. He was keeper of Dumbarton Castle, and one of the Parliament (1371) which fixed the settlement of the crown on his grand-nephew, John, Earl of Carric. In 1373, Robert Danielston, knight, had a crown charter of Danzelston, a £40 land, and Finlawiston, in the barony of Renfrew and shire of Lanark, to be held in free barony; and he had a grant of Staneley, in Paisley, from Robert III., in 1391. On his decease, the barony was divided into those of Danielston-Cuningham, and Danielston-Maxwell, by the marriage of his two daugh-ters, Margaret and Elizabeth, co-heiresses, the former to Sir Robert Cuningham of Kilmaurs, and the latter to Sir Robert Maxwell of Calderwood. Here, from a field which is called Kite-hill, we survey the scene we are leaving: the villas, and neat houses and cottages, and the square tower of the Parish Church, forming a prominent object in the landscape. The green vale of Kilmalcolm is seen stretching down from Dunrod hill, and Duchal moors, to Bridge of Weir, and forms a very pretty and pleasant picture. Here, nearest us, is the vale of the Gryfe; there rises the rough form of Clachers, or Cairncuran hill; beyond lies the vale of the Green water;

in the hollow, surrounded by ample plantations, stands Duchal New House (Sir Michael Shaw Stewart, Bart.) The white farm houses, surrounded with a few trees, give a variegated aspect to the valley, and the heathy mosses and moors of Duchal, terminated by the Misty Law, the highest point in Renfrewshire, shut it in, as it were, from the outer world. As we proceed farther up our country road, we linger to pluck the blue-bells waving gaily by the wayside, and think what a pleasant spot this would be for a residence, where one would have always pure air, clear water springing from the rock, and a commanding view of valley, hills, and moors. Some way further up we come to a villa building in a pleasant little green hollow at the foot of a rock. Here we turn off the road, and climb some of the neighbouring heights to have a view of the Highland mountains, which we can descry all the way round from Kilpatrick to Cowal, Ben Lomond and Ben Ledi towering above the rest. From some of the heights in the neighbourhood, it is said, Cruachan Ben can be seen with the aid of a glass. We now retrace our steps to the village, through green fields and broomy knolls.

Our next walk shall be to Garner's Braes, on the Finlayston road. Leaving the village, our way winds gradually up the hill. As we go we observe the bare whin cropping out in some places, here as everywhere else throwing its bold face towards the west. This is accounted for in the following way:- It is supposed that at one time all Scotland was under water, and that a current swept across it from west to east, denuding the western faces of the cliffs, and casting banks of sand and gravel to the east. The faces of the low crags hereabout all show a bold face to the west. On our left we pass the house of W. Brown, Esq., M.D., and, wending our

upland way among hills and farms and copsewood, we
begin to descry the tops of the Argyleshire hills rising
heavily against the sky. Soon we reach the turn of the road
at Garner's Braes, and are greeted with a prospect of great
magnificence and beauty. A great portion of the counties of
Stirling, Dumbarton, and Argyle lies beneath our gaze.
There are the dark masses of the Kilpatrick hills to the east,
the vale of Leven extending inwards; the shores of the Firth,
Cardross and Helensburgh, and the wild and rugged ranges
of Argyleshire hills. Beneath us, in the setting sun, lies the
peaceful glen of Finlayston stretching downwards to the
shore. After admiring to our heart's content this fine scene,
we retrace our steps to the village.

Other short Walks may be recommended, such as that
down the Bridge-of-Weir road, and that along the Port-
Glasgow road. A pleasant hour may also be spent in going
round the Barclaven hills, ascending by the ravine above the
Manse. On the heights here the innkeepers in old times used
always to light a bonfire of wood, peats, coal, and tar
barrels, on the eve of the Midsummer fair. Here is the Glen
Moss, or Goakhouse bog, from which the villagers of yore
had the right of casting their peats. By going along the
heights fine views may be got both of the village and valley.

*   *   *   *   *

KILMALCOLM - ECCLESIASTIC.

THE word "Kil," which is found in the names of many parishes in Ireland and the West of Scotland, is said to be derived from celta, the Latin for a cell, or the rude dwelling of the early missionaries of the Scottish Church of Ireland. That was in the golden age of the Irish, before they had abjured the race-name Scot, and thirled themselves to His Holiness the Pope. Columba's disciples went far and near over Albion (Scotland), and to the Saxon settlers south of the Tweed, where the Gaelic was spoken. Their churches, built of wattles, rude and homely structures, were called "kils," or cells, and some godly man's name was usually added--so, Kilbarchan, Church of St. Barchan; Kilpeter, now Houston, Church of St. Peter; Kilmalcolm, &c. In regard to Kilmalcolm, it is a moot point whether it means the Church of Columba, or 'the Church of Malcolm III., one of the Scottish kings. Cosmo Innes says:- "The ancient Church of Kilmacolm is said, but without any authority, to have been dedicated to King Malcolm III. There can be little doubt that it was one of the numerous Churches dedicated to St. Columba." On the other hand, the Fasti Ecclesiae Scoticanae, a, very good authority, says:--"The Church was dedicated to Malcolm III. of Scotland." The earliest form of the word, as it is written in the Chartulary of Paisley, "Kylmalcolm," favours the latter supposition; the common pronunciation of "Kilmacolm," the former. In any case it is plain that, about the seventh or eighth century, or even much later, Gaelic was the language spoken all over the West of Scotland, both Highlands and Lowlands.

It appears from a donation by Baldwin de Bigres, vice-comes de Lanerk (which then included Renfrew), of the kirk of Innerkyp to the Monastery of Paisley, that the monks of that Abbey then possessed the kirks of Strath-Grief, by the donation of Walter, the son of Alan, Steward to the King of Scotland. This was in the reign of Malcolm IV. There would be a church here at that time, as there has been ever since, and which is now the Parish Church. The grant of Walter, the son of Alan, was confirmed to them by name, by Florence, bishop-elect, 1202-7. In 1227 the cure was served by a vicar pensioner, who had 100s. yearly from the altarage. Hugh de Parcliner, perpetual vicar of Kilmalcolm, is witness to a charter granted by Donald Makgilcriste, lord of Tarbard, granting to the monks of Paisley the right of cutting wood within all his territory, for the building and use of their monastery, after the middle of the 13th century; and on Monday next, after the feast of the Purification, in 1303, Sir Hugh de Sprakelin, vicar of Kilmalcolm, lent his seal to another ticate-a deed granted at Paisley by Roger, son of Lawrence, clerk of Stewardton, whose seal was not suffi-ciently known. In the Libelus Tax. Rey. Scot. the rectory of Kilmalcolm is valued at £40. It was let for 200 merks at the time of the Reformation. The vicarage is taxed in Baiamund according to a value of £53 6s. 8d. It was let at the time of the Reformation for 50 merks. Its glebe was of two acres.

At Westside, on a farm now called Chapel, and not very far from the old Castle of Duchal, there was a chapel on the Greenwater, which appears to have been endowed by the family of Lyle, the lords of the manor. Master David Stonyer, hermit of the chapel of Syde, is a witness to a deed in 1555. There is now no vestige of this old chapel remaining.

The following is a list of the ministers of Kilmalcolm, so far as known:-

1227. A vicar Pensioner, who had 100s. yearly from the Altarage.

1295. Hugo de Parcliner, Perpetuus Vicarius of Kylmacolme.

1261. William, Capellano de Kylmalcolm.

1295. Dominus Hugo, Chapellano Vicaris de Kylmalcolm.

1303. Domini Hugonis de Sparkclyn, Vicar of Kylmalcolm.

1555. Magister David Stonyer, Hermit of the Chapel of Syde, in Kylmalcolm.

1560. Umphray Cunninghame, Vicar of Kilmalcolm, at the Reformation.

AFTER THE REFORMATION.
(From Fasti Ecclesiae Scoticanae.)

1574. James Craw, Lochquhinzeoch, was also under his charge, with a stipend of £6 13s. 4d.; continued in 1579.

1578. Robert Cuik, translated from Kilbarchan; continued in 1579.

1580. Archibald Spittal, took the degree of A.M. at the Univ. of Glasgow in 1553; continued in 1586; and was translated to Kilmaronock before 1558.

1588. David Conynghame, A.M., had his degree from the Univ. of Glasgow in 1586; he was named a member of the Court of High Commission, 15th July, 1619; continued, 27th March, 1628; but was resident in Lochwinnoch, 26th March, 1646.

1629. Alexander Hamilton, A.M., probably third son of Claud Hamilton of Little Earnock, attained his degree at the Univ. of Edinburgh, 23d July, 1625. Ordained and admitted at Glasgow, 15th April, 1629 - translated to Haddington same year.

1630. Ninian Campbell, A.M., a native of the Highlands, and skilful in their language, was laureated at the Univ. of Glasgow in 1619; passed trials before the Presbytery, and was admitted on or after 1st April, 1630; appointed by the Presbytery "to gee to the Armie nowe in England and supplie them as minister till he were liberat," 1644; translated to Roseneath, 20th Feb., 1651.

1651. Thomas Hall, A.M., formerly of Erskine; received for the time, 28th May; continued, 12th July, 1654; but returned to his former charge at Larne, Ireland, where he died in 1695, aged 75, in the 49th year of his ministry. He was respected as a person of solid learning and judgment, integrity and piety, as well as of constancy as a sufferer for the truth, yet modest and humble."

1655. James Alexander, A.M., graduated at the University of Glasgow in 1653; called in February, and ordained in March, 1655; deprived by the Acts of Parliament, 11th June, and of Privy Council, 1st October, 1662. He was accused of preaching and baptizing irregularly, and for so doing was called to Ayr in March, 1669. He died of fever in the same year, aged about 34. "He was eminent for piety, and a considerable scholar, singular for gravity, and of most obliging temper." His wife, Mary Maxwell, took his death so much to heart that she died little more than a year after him. By her he had a son, who became laird of Blackhouse.

1663. Andrew Abercrombie, A.M., a native of Aberdeen, took his degree from the Univ. and King's college there, 13th July, 1658; for not hearing of whom Porterfield of Duchal was fined £500 sterling in July, 1664. Translated to Innernochtie, or Strathdon, after 21st of said month.

1665. John Irvine, A.M., of the ancient family of Drum, took his degree at the Univ. of Glasgow in 1658: passed trials before the Presbytery, and got a testimonial, 2d March, 1665, for ordination; the Commissioners of the Western Shires were instructed by the Privy Council, 7th July, 1676, "to take trial anent the abuse done to him both in the Church and house of Finlayston." He was translated to Peterculter in 1673.

1672. Patrick Simpson, formerly of Renfrew; indulged by the Privy Council, 3d September. He was accused, in 1674, of baptizing children belonging to other congregations; in 1677 he forwarded a contribution of money to Peden and the other prisoners in the Bass;", and, being accused of breaking his confinement, and not appearing in Nov., 167, 8, the Privy Council declared the Church vacant, 16th May, 1679. He returned to Renfrew in 1687.

1679. David Barclay, A.M., nephew of Fothringham of Powrie, presented by John, Earl of Glencairn, in Aug., 1677; installed 24th Sept., 1679; died in Julie, 1650.

1682. James Gadderar, A.M., attained his degree at the Univ: of Glasgow, 20th July, 1675; having passed trials before Presbytery there, he was recommended, 23d March, 13s, for licence; presented by John, Earl of Glencairn, 23d Dec., same year; was admitted 15th and 16th Jan., 1683; deprived by the people, and deserted his charge at the Revolution. He was afterwards consecrated as Bishop of the Non-Jurant Church at London, 24th Feb., 1712; and was allotted the diocese of Aberdeen. He died in Feb., 1733.

1688. James Hay, A. M.; ordained 16th Jan., 1688. Translated to Kilsyth, 29th Sept., 1692.

1693. James Brisbane; ordained 21st Nov., 1693. Translated to Stirling in Sept., 1703.

1706. Robert Maxwell; called 13th Feb., and ordained 30th April, 1706; died, 18th Feb., 1735.

1737. John Fleming, son of Mr. W. Fleming, minister of Houston; called 9th Jan., and ordained 23d Jan., 1737; had D.D. from the Univ. of Glasgow, 8th Dec., 1786; and died, 30th June, 1787, in his 76th year, and of his ministry the 51st. He was distinguished for his talents, knowledge, conduct, and piety, which commanded universal esteem.

1788. John Brown; licensed by the Presbytery of Glasgow, 12th May, 1781; became assistant to the Rev. Thomas Maxwell, of Stewarton; presented by James, Earl of Glencairn; and ordained, 8th May, 1788; died, 12th Nov., 1817, in the 69th year of his age, and 31st of his ministry.

1819. Rob. Cameron; licensed by the Presbytery of Glasgow, 5th Sept., 1804; presented by Dr. William Anderson, physician in Glasgow, in Feb., 1818; ordained, 6th May, 1819; got a new church built in 1834, and died, 20th June, 1842.

1843. Thomas Brydson, minister till 1855.

1858. Alexander Leek, the present minister.

There is a tradition in the parish, that when the last curate was put away, the folks gathered with kail-stocks, bindweed, and other missiles, to drive him from his abode. One rustic, more wroth than his neighbours, carried aloft a huge pitchfork, with which, with direful threats, he declared that he would "stick the curate." That individual, however, having a shrewd guess of the intentions of his flock, fled away, and that so hastily that a joint of beef roasting for his dinner was left on the spit before the fire. This was elevated on the prongs of the pitchfork, and paraded in triumph round the village.

Several of the parishioners of Kilmalcolm wrote to Rutherford when at Anwoth, asking his counsel on various questions. In his reply he gives so judicious advice that we cannot do better than quote a great part of his letter:-

TO THE PARISHIONERS OF KILMACOLME.

Worthy and well-beloved in Christ Jesus, our Lord, - Grace, Mercy, and Peace be to you. Your letter could not come to my hand in a greater throng of business than I am now pressed with at this time, when our Kirk requireth the public help of us all; yet I cannot but answer. the heads of both your letters, with provision that ye choose after this a fitter time of writing. 1. I would not have you pitch upon me as the man able by letters to answer doubts of this kind, while there are in your bounds men of such great parts, most able for this work. I know the best are unable; yet it pleaseth that Spirit of Jesus to blow his sweet wind through a piece of dry stick, that the empty reed may keep no glory to itself; but a minister can make no such wind as this to blow-he is scarce able to lend it a passage through him. 2. Know that the wind of this Spirit hath a time when it bloweth sharp, and pierceth so strongly that it would blow through an iron door, and this is commonly rather under suffering for Christ than at any other time. Sick children get of Christ's pleasant things to play them withal, because Jesus is most tender of the sufferer, for lie was a sufferer himself. Oh, if I had but the leavings and the drawing of the by-board of the sufferer's table! But I leave this to answer yours.

First, ye write that God's vows are lying on you, and security strong and sib to nature stealing oil you who are weak. I answer:--I. Till we be in heaven, the best have heavy heads, as is evident (Cant, v. 1, Psal. xxx. 6, Job xxix. 18, Matt. xxvi. 33). Nature is a sluggard, and loveth not the labour of religion: therefore rest should not be taken till we know the disease to be over and in the way of turning, and that it is like a fever past the cool. And the quietness, and the calms of the faith of the victory over corruption would be entertained in place of security, so that if I sleep, I would desire to sleep faith's sleep in Christ's bosom. Know also, none that sleep sound can seriously complain of sleepiness, sorrow for a slumbering soul is a token of some watchfulness of spirit. But this is soon turned into wantonness (as grace in us too often is absurd); therefore, our waking must be watched over, else sleep will even grow out of watching; and there is as much need to watch over grace as to watch over sin. Full men will soon sleep, and sooner than hungry men. 3. For your weakness to keep off security, that like a thief stealeth upon you, I would say two things. (1) To want complaints of weakness is for heaven and angels that never sinned, not for Christians in Christ's camp on earth. I think our weakness maketh us the Church of the redeemed ones, and Christ's field that the Mediator should labour in. If there were no diseases on earth, there needed no physicians on earth; if Christ had cried down weakness, he might have cried down his own calling; but weakness is our Mediator's world. Sin is Christ's only, only fair and market. No man should rejoice at weakness and diseases; but I think we may have a sort of gladness at boils and sores, because without them Christ's fingers, as a slain Lord, should never have touched our skin. I dare not thank myself, but I dare thank God's depth of wise providence, that I have an errand in me, while I live, for Christ to come and visit me, and bring with him his drugs and his balm. 0 how sweet is it for a sinner to put his weakness in Christ's strengthening hand, and to fatten a sick soul upon such a physician, and to lay weakness before him, to weep upon him, and to plead and pray; weakness can speak and cry when we have not a tongue (Ezek. xvi. 6) - "And when I passed by thee, and saw thee polluted in thine own blood, I said unto thee, when thou wast in thy blood, Live." The Kirk could not speak one word to Christ then, but blood and guiltiness out of measure spoke, and drew oat of Christ pity, and a word of life and love. (2) For weakness, we have it that we may employ Christ's strength because of our weakness. Weakness is to make us the strongest things-that is, when having no strength of our own, we are carried upon Christ's shoulders, and walk, as it were, upon his legs. If your sinful weakness swell up to the clouds, Christ's strength will swell up to the sun, and far above the heaven of heavens. (2) Ye tell me that there is need of counsel for strengthening of new beginners. I can say little to that, who am not well begun myself; but I know honest beginnings are nourished by him, even by lovely Jesus, who never yet put out a poor man's dim candle who was wrestling betwixt light and darkness. I am sure if new beginners would urge themselves upon Christ, and press their souls upon him, and importune him for a draught, of his sweet love, they could not come wrong to Christ. Come once in upon the right nick and step of his lovely love, and I defy you to get free of him again. If any beginners fall off Christ, and miss him, they never lighted upon Christ as Christ; it was but an idol like Jesus they took for him. (3) When ye complain of a dead ministry in your bounds, ye are to remember that the Bible among you is the contract of marriage, and the manner of Christ's conveying his love to your heart is not so absolutely dependent upon even living preaching, as that there is no conversion at all, no life of Cod, but that which is tied to a man's lips. The daughters of Jerusalem have (lone often that which the watchmen could not do. Make Christ your minister; he can woo a soul at a dyke-side in the field; be needeth not us, howbeit the flock be obliged to seek him in the shepherd's tent. Hunger of Christ's making may thrive, even under stewards who mind not the feeding of the flock. 0 blessed soul that can leap over a man, and look above a pulpit up to Christ, who can preach home to the heart, howbeit we are all dead and rotten! (4) So, to complain of yourself as to justify God is right, and providing you justify his spirit in yourself; for men seldom advocate against Satan's work and sin in themselves, but against God's work in themselves. Some of the people of God slander God's grace in their souls, as some wretches use to do who complain and murmur of want. I have nothing (say they), all is gone, the ground yieldeth but weeds and windlestraws; whereas their fat harvest, and their money in bank, maketh them liars

I recommend to you conference and prayer at private meetings; for warrant whereof see Isa. ii. 3, &c. Many coals make a good fire, and this is a part of the Communion of Saints. I must entreat you, and your Christian acquaintances in the parish, to remember me to God in your prayers, and my flock and ministry, and my transportation and removal from this place, which I fear at this Assembly. And be earnest with God for our mother Kirk. For want of time I have put you all in one letter. The rich grace of our Lord Jesus Christ be with you all. Yours in his sweet Lord Jesus,

S. R.

ANWOTH, Aug. 5, 1639.

*   *   *   *   *

OTHER CHURCHES IN KILMALCOLM.

REFORMED PRESBYTERIAN.

THE Macmillanites, or Reformed Presbyterians, had a place of worship at Kilmalcolm for many years. The Church was built here as a central spot for their members, some of whom came from great distances, from Argyle, and from Dalry in Ayr. On communion seasons part of the preaching was always in the open. air, and vast crowds used to assemble from the neighbouring parishes. But latterly the custom of vast gatherings was given up.

The ministers have been-

1. Thomas Henderson, ordained in the open air at the mound called Gryfe Castle, near Bridge-of-Weir, in 1787. A church was built at Kilmalcolm the same year. He died in the year 1823.

2. William Maclachlan, ordained in 1825; removed with the congregation to Port-Glasgow in 1856, when the church at Kilmalcolm was sold.

BAPTISTS

For nearly 70 years a meeting of Baptists was kept up in the parish, which was conducted by laymen, the chief of whom were--John Laird of Middlepenny; James Gardner, Milltoun; John Gardner, Milltoun; William Stevenson, Wardwell; James Gardner, jun., Milltoun. On the lamented death of the last, by a railway accident, the meetings, which used to be held in an old school-room, were discontinued.

FREE CHURCH.

Was built and opened in 1845. Was supplied by various preachers, among whom were--Thos. Gordon, formerly minister at Falkirk; James Gordon, taken to Young Street, Glasgow, 1856; Allan Ferguson; and Alexander Gordon. Was discontinued, and the church sold, in 1859.

UNITED PRESBYTERIAN CHURCH.

The first Secession Church in the West of Scotland was nursed at Killochrie's, on the Greenwater, in this parish, during last century; but the church was ultimately built at Burnt Shiels, in Kilbarchan, and was the mother of most of the Secession, now U.P., Churches in the district. The present United Presbyterian congregation arose in 1858. Rev. James E. Fyfe was ordained minister in 1860. The church was built in 1861-62. It was opened by Professor Eadie, of Glasgow, who preached from Psalm cxlix. 2 - "Let the children of Zion be joyful in their king."

*   *   *   *   *

KILMALCOLM AS A PLACE OF RESIDENCE AND FOR SUMMER VISITORS.

Hackney'd in business, wearied at that oar
Which thousands, once fast chain'd to, quit no more,
Put which, when life, at ebb, runs weak and low,
All wish, or seem to wish, they could forego;
The statesman, lawyer, merchant, man of trade,
Pants for the refuge of some rural shade,
Where, all his long anxieties forgot,
Amid the charms of a sequestered spot,
Or recollected only to gild o'er,
And add a smile to what was sweet before,
He may possess the joys he thinks he sees,
Lay his old age upon the lap of ease,
Improve the remnant of his wasted span,
And, having liv'd a trifler, die a man.

Cowper.

THE poet in these lines sets forth to us the longing of a man of business, immersed in the whirl of worldly concerns, for some quiet scene in the country, to which he might retire and spend his old age in peace. When he wrote, men of business found it impossible to carry on their business in the city, and yet to live in the country: they must live where they toiled. But the steam-boat and the railway have altered all that; and now the men of business of Greenock, Port-Glasgow, Paisley, and Glasgow can have their villas all along the shores of the Clyde, and in many a pleasant nook of the country. Summer visitors, too, are beginning to find that more health and happiness are to be got by residing for a month or so in one place in the country, than by a hurried rush from place to place in quest of remarkable scenes. To both these classes, as well as to the tourist, the vale and village of Kilmalcolm offer many attractions. The stream that year by year sets down the water is beginning to pick out other spots, where equal or superior benefits to the constitution are to be reaped. For some the "saut water" may be too strong, to whom the smell of the heather, and' the rustle of green leaves would bring back the fading roses to the cheeks: and in the selection of a country dwelling place, or place for summer residence, no man can fail to take chiefly into consideration the healthfulness of the locality, since that is the main point for him in leaving town at all. Some of the old villagers, before the railway was made, were wont to complain that "thae railways had ruined our toun completely;" but since the railway was made the amenity and beauty of the locality are becoming better known, and the consequence is that residences are rapidly being erected, and a rush of visitors in quest of health and pleasure has set in, which there is every reason to suppose will go on increasing. Kilmalcolm has indeed very superior attractions and advantages. 1st. It enjoys easy communication by good roads and railway with the great centres of trade, Glasgow, Paisley, and Greenock, so that it can be reached by driving, or by rail, or on foot. 2nd. The quiet pastoral beauty of the vale, forming as it does the upper part of the valley of the Gryfe water, which was anciently called Strathgryfe, and being surrounded and, as it were, shut out of the world by moors and low heathery hills. This gives it a special character of its own; and for those who seek retirement, which at a short space may be exchanged for the bustle of Greenock or Paisley, we could fancy no meeter spot. In the moors around the hollow vale rise the Gryfe, the Green water, and the Duchal, and each of these streams has a green vale stretching along its banks. 3rd. The situation of the village, which lies in a nook of the valley, and looks towards the south and west. A mansion placed on one of those heights around the village would both command a most extensive prospect, and be a commanding object in the landscape. 4th. But, above all, the salubrity of the place presents the highest attraction. This, after all, is really the most important point for those who seek the pleasures of rural retirement. The longevity of the inhabitants of this favoured locality is an undoubted fact, and has been commented on by various other writers. That we do not speak without book on this most important point we shall prove conclusively by quoting the remarks of two writers, who both wrote before Kilmalcolm was so much known. The author of *A Run Through Kilmalcolm,* writing in 1856, says: "The well-known salubrity of the place holds out great inducements to invalids to visit it. Here are fine air, pure water, wholesome food, rural walks, retirement, and cheap living. The following are the vital statistics of the inhabitants: - The population of the village is under two hundred. Of these there are at present alive and active eight persons above eighty years of age, fourteen above seventy, and eighteen above sixty--that is, forty individuals whose united ages amount to 2,220 years. From whatever cause this longevity arises, these are simple facts. One of the octogenarians is the grave-digger, and yet he goes about his melancholy but necessary employment with the activity of a youth. For many long years has he performed his sad office:--

> "Scarce a skull casts up
> But well he knew its owner, and can tell
> Some passage in his life."

The late lamented poet, and writer too, Hugh Macdonald, in his charming work, *Days at the Coast,* has noted the same fact:-- "Longevity is common in this out of the way community, and we are informed that many of the inhabitants have passed the allotted threescore and ten by a goodly number of years. On congratulating an elderly lady on her residence in such a long-lived locality, a buxom kimmer who overhears us exclaims, 'Ay, ay, we may get a guile bit o' the tether here, but we a' dee at last, as weel as the folk in the warld:' referring of course to the popular saying of 'Out of the world and into Kilmalcolm.' We were assured by a minister of the gospel that he had never known a place where there were so many folk between seventy and eighty; and that he had known invalids brought from Greenock, or Port-Glasgow, so weak that they bad to be carried into the house, in a fortnight going about among the hills. There is a family of three belonging to the parish whose united ages amount to 279 years; the eldest of whom, now approaching the hundred, is yet able to sew a white seam as well as any practised needlewoman. We may state that in the possession of this family is a curious relic of Rob Roy, viz., his horn snuff mull, once chased with silver, but now bare. They had likewise a kind of mill for grinding snuff, with which that hero, when he was not in his heroic keys, was wont to solace himself by grinding taddy; but that is lost. We are assured by a gentleman, who has made the question his study, that Kilmalcolm is some degrees warmer than Glasgow; and he accounts for it in this way that whenever there is sunshine the country gets the benefit of it, while it often takes some hours for the sun's rays to pierce through the fogs of the city. The friable nature of the soil also allows the rain water to be carried off at once, and prevents the dampness of the atmosphere.

The following extract from the Greenock Telegraph of February 28, 1872, confirms all we have here said: "We direct attention to the Registrar-General's report just published as to the salubrity of the parish [of Kilmalcolm] and the exceeding small death-rate: 16 to the 1,000. This favourable statement will doubtless add to the increasing reputation of the place as a healthy resort, and already houses are being quickly taken up for the coming season."

The pure air which is here enjoyed will go a long way to account for the salubrity of the place. To this add clear springs of water, a moderate competence with easy toil, and a simple life, and we think we have enumerated the elements of longevity. Dwellers in large towns and cities are beginning to recognise the fact that they must pay for their privileges with abridgement of life, and that a residence in the country is a happy alternative and tonic for the wear and tear of life in a busy town.

*   *   *   *   *

A DAY AMANG THE HEATHER.

REN-FREW, or Rein-fraoch, the heather part, was not ill-named when Strathgryfe, the older name, was laid aside; for in no part of this strath will you go far till you come to the bonnie blooming heather, or to bare scaurs of the whin, or on low-lying mosses in the dale. Whether we take the road to Barclaven braes, or the stony wilds of Cairn-curran hill, or on the heathery and mossy fells of Duchal moors, or to the Misty-law--in any part of that wild tract which was formerly known to the good monks of Paisley as "the Moors," when they speak, in the Chartulary of the Abbey, of Innerkyp as lying "extra mores," we will find plenty to please the eye, and refresh the weary machine of the body. Much moor and heath has been torn in since the time of the good monks, as Thomas the Rhymer prophesied of old, and in his prophesies fore-boded but little hope of the fine visions which are sometimes dangled before the e'en of the poor--

> "The waters shall wax, the woods shall wene,
>   Hill and moss shall be torn in,
>   But the bannock will never be braider."

Last century was a great time for inclosing fields with stone dykes and fences, when agriculture began to be studied, on the quiet settlement of the country after Culloden; but here, as in all upland places, much land will never cultivate, and must always be left to Nature.

Let us, then, have a day amongst the heather. Say there are three or four of us. One gets his fishing tackle in order; another has his Botany, wherein to seek out the names of all the plants we will meet with; and a third has his pencil and sketch book. Some homely fare of bread and cheese, or a sandwich, must be taken as lunch, for hills are hungry places to go to, and we don't wish to be like Donald in the song of the Ettrick Shepherd--

> "Donald gaed up the hill cauld an' hungry;
> Donald cam doun the hill cauld an' angry."

But to the uninitiated we may state that the simpler and homelier the food the better; and if the walk and exertion do not make it palatable it will be a wonder voluptuous feasts are not sought by those who delight in our homely, simple, and health-giving joys. Here we are out on the moor: how peaceful the hollow vale sleeps beneath in the sunny light, its white farm hamlets gleaming among the trees, and rich with green fields or golden waving corn. How clear and bright the blue sky above, and how fresh and pure the air. What pleasure to breath it, after being used to the close and heavy vapours of our wynds and closes. Here is a pure, caller, crystal spring rising in the moor, welling out amid a little strip of grass, which its waters nourish amid the surrounding world of heath; it is cool and refreshing. Yonder is a small lochan, in a hollow, with stunted alder bushes on its sides, and water plants on its surface, with the exquisite flower of the evergreen bogbean, "wasting its sweetness on the desert air." Hark how cheerily the laverock sings his lilt in the lift overhead, soaring high aboon the ferny brae, where the brackens wave, and the junipers and the blaeberries grow! Or yonder, from the dark waters of the Gryfe, rises the heron, with his great flapping wings: or here we start the timid hare, or a covey of whirring moorfowl. Or deeper in the moors and mosses we shall see around us but the wild heather, with a cairn rising here and there amid it, and the flocks of sheep browsing on the hillside; and hear the whaup, the shy and lonely abider on the moors, piping his shrill cry, or the wild ducks rising from the marsh or mere with spattering wings. Here, on the sunny brae, we will discuss our frugal meal, lay out our plans, where we shall go each his several way, and where unite before returning to our lodging or to mine inn. Then the fisher holds off to the stream, the Duchal, or the Green water, or the Gryfe, to wile the finny tribes out of their pools; the botanist for some known habitat of herbs and flowers that bloom "by bank and burn;" the artist to sketch some hoary ruin or ancient-looking cottage. On returning at gloamin', we rejoice to compare notes of our day's doings, and make the larder pay over tea for the frugal fare of our noonday meal. Such a mode of spending a day, as we take it, will give us a new stock of health, many little: incidents and pleasant adventures which it will be a source of joy to call to mind afterwards, and will lift the mind for awhile from the cares of sordid money-getting: that very necessary art of heaping up of gold and silver, houses and lands, stocks, and railway shares, which, albeit a very needful and honourable art, may be overdone, and defeat its own end by too eagerly following it. For the end of all toil should be a healthy soul in a healthy body; and small profit has he who has heaped up much means of life, and yet has neglected to nurse and cherish the life itself, or has lavishly squandered it away on lawless and vicious delights, losing the substance in pursuit of the shadow. For it is beginning again to be known that simple and homely joys, which may be said to be within the reach of all, are far to the fore with high-spiced pleasures, towards the votaries and loud-tongued praises of which the world begins to grow deaf, like Sir Joshua Reynolds to foolish talkers on the fine arts--

> "When they talk of their Raphaels, Correggios, and stuff,
> He shifted his trumpet, and only took snuff."

        *   *   *   *   *

A VISIT TO DUCHAL CASTLE.

Of all the clans that grace fair Renfrew's soil,
The first in pow'r appears the potent Lyle,
Whose blood with graceful Eglinton's still blends,
In Pollok's veins and Houston's still descends.
The Clyde.

THE ruins of Duchal Castle, the ancient seat of the Lords Lyle, and after them of the Porterfields of that ilk, stand at the distance of about two miles from the village, in the vale of the Greenwater. Thither on a fine mild summer day we bend our course. Crossing the railway, which here makes a pretty deep cutting through the whinstone rock, we soon come to the Gryfe, here a small dark stream fringed with a few bushes. It is farther down swollen by the Duchal, and, joining with the Black Cart, falls into the Clyde at the Water-neb. The vale through which it flows, and the whole district, bore in former times the name of Strathgryfe, while it yet formed a part of the great shire of Lanark, which it did till the reign of Robert III., who erected it into a distinct sheriffdom, to which was given the name of Renfrew.

Ascending a rising ground which slopes downwards from Clachers' hill (or Stony hill as the word means in Gaelic), we come into the vale of the Green-water, a pleasant valley, stretching east and west, between the aforesaid hill on the one side and Duchal moors on the other. We turn off the road, and passing a farm steading, come to the Old Place. Duchal Castle, now only crumbling ruins, stands on a rocky promontory at the confluence of the Green-water and the Duchal. It lies in the hollow of the vale, and is not seen till the visitor is close upon it. Now consisting of only crumbling ivied walls and grassy mounds, from its extent and situation it has evidently been at one time a very strong place, and well nigh impregnable, fortified both by nature and art. The natural strength of the place, from the rocky nature of the site, and the two mountain streams surrounding it on three sides, had been increased by a careful adaptation of the walls to the necessities of defence: and doubtless, on the west or entrance side, there had been fosse, and wall, and drawbridge; though all indications of these are now obliterated. A row of ancient lime trees in a neighbouring park, and the name of the farm beside the castle, Muthill, seem to bear some indication of the old glories; the former telling of his Lordship's park, and the latter of his Moat or Meet-hill, where the barons used to give their judicial decisions, surrounded by crowds of their retainers. The ruins were formerly of greater extent, but part of them were removed for the construction of a summer-house at the new house of Duchal which stands about two miles farther down at the confluence of the Duchal and the Gryfe, and is a large and handsome edifice, well planted and sheltered by woods, and was built in 1768. In removing the ruins on this occasion a large quantity of bones were found in an upper apartment.

The great barony of Duchall, which for many ages was the chief property and place of residence of the ancient and now almost extinct family of Lyle Lord Lyle, and afterwards became the property of the great family of Porterfield of that ilk, was of great extent, situated in the heart of the parish, on both sides of the Gryfe, but chiefly inland from it.

The first mention of the family of Lyle (who are said to have been originally a West Highland family, and to derive their name from L'isle. An eminent local antiquary holds on the other hand that the castle surrounded on three sides by the stream, and on the fourth by a fosse which was crossed by a drawbridge, is the Insula meant; and that they took their name from the island on which the fort was built. This seems likely.) occurs in the grant which "Baldwin de Bigres," Sheriff of Lanark, which then included Renfrew, made to the Monks of Paisley, of the Church of Innerkip, when "Radulphus de Insula, Dominus de Duchal" is mentioned as a witness to several donations to that Abbey, an. 1243, in King Alexander II.'s time. Sir Robert Lyll, of Duchal, being a baron of an ample fortune, was raised to the dignity of Lord Lyll, of Duchal, by King James II., in the year 1445. Robert Lord Lyll, his son, was Justiciar of Scotland, in the reign of King James IV. John Lord Lyll alienated most part of the lordship of Duchal, in the year 1544, to John Porterfield of that ilk, with the special consent of James, Master of Lyll, his eldest son and apparent heir: which James, the last of the family, died without succession about the year 1556. But there seems to have been some dubiety about the alienation, for in the year 1599 William Porterfield, by the decision of umpires, paid a sum of money to Sir Neil Montgomery, of Langshaw, in satisfaction of his claim to the lordship of Duchal, as heir and nearest of line to John Lord Lyll, and James, Master of Lyll.

The family of Porterfield, which then came into possession of the estate, took their surname and designation from
their ancient possession on the river Cart, which is named
Porterfield. Allan de Porter is mentioned as one of the
hostages for the liberation of William the Lion. In the reign
of King Alexander III., anno. 1262, John de Porter was a
witness to the donation of the Kirk of Dundonald, by
Alexander, High Steward of Scotland to the Monks of
Paisley. John Porterfield of that ilk, who succeeded to the
family estate in 1540, being a person of great learning,
added considerable purchases to the family estate, in special
that of Duchal, from John Lord Lyll, in the year 1544. He
deceased in 1575; and was succeeded by his son, William.
His descendants held the estate for 300 years, and on the
death of the last laird, it came, after a long law-suit, into the
possession of Sir Michael Shaw Stewart, Bart.

The castle was once besieged by the rival family of
Glencairn, but such was its strength that the assailants could
make no way. At last, after several of his men had been
slain, Glencairn was allowed to enter in a friendly manner,
but no sooner had he done so than he took forcible possession of the place with his retainers, from which he was only
dislodged by an order of King James the Sixth, dated 27th
August, 1578. A few years after, though he did not appear
openly in the matter, Glencairn had influence enough to get
a party of Highlanders from Argyle to harry the estate. They
crossed in their boats at the Cloch, and coming down upon
the glen by night swept it bare of cattle and sheep. Tradition
says that they fired in at a window at the farm of Dipenny,
and killed a bairn. Next morning,

> The farmer rose to yoke the steer,
> The steer was stown awa',
> The maiden rose to milk the kye,
> But toom was ilka sta'.

The laird of Duchal gathered his men, and followed hard after the Catherans, who made all haste with their plunder, and had actually got some of the beasts into the boats, when the pursuers came up with them, and after interchanging a few blows recovered the whole of their cattle; and took eight or nine of the marauders prisoners, who were in due time tried, condemned, and hanged in the Grassmarket of Edinburgh.

A more pleasing reminiscence of this fine old ruin is that here sundry of the persecuted adherents of the Covenant found a shelter from their ruthless foes. There is an eminence in the neighbouring moss where the Covenanters were wont to meet for worship.

We were told the following story of the times of the persecution. One day when the lady of the castle and all the domestics, save the cook, were away at a neighbouring eminence to hear some of the proscribed preachers, there came a travelling woman to the gate of the castle, and asked admission and shelter for the night. The cook thought she might admit her, for the family were known for hospitality. She bade the woman come in and sit down in the kitchen. By chance after some time she happened to look at her sleeve, and what was her horror to see the cuffs of a scarlet coat peeping out. She knew now that this was some soldier of the informer class, and feared her lady and her master would be undone by the imposition of ruinous fines which was sure to follow his report. In this desperate emergency she bethought her of a lavish hospitality, and plied the travelling woman with ale, usquebaugh, and brandy, till, when the party returned, he was blind and deaf to all beneath the moon. The lady being informed of the case, the seeming travelling woman was solemnly lifted up, and deposited in a shallow part of the neighbouring stream, out of which he is supposed to have escaped safely, as he was never more heard of.

After musing for a while among the ruins, and admiring the beauty which summer gives to the leafy woods, we take our way back to the village. On our return we have a fine peep of the modern mansion of Duchal, standing in the hollow, well sheltered by woods and plantations. An excellent view of the village is also obtained, and very pleasant and picturesque does it look, with the now descending sun casting a flood of light on the village and the church and the neat houses clustering around it. How peaceful and quiet, too, the vale looks. But the shades of evening descend, and warn us to quicken our steps; and in a little while we are comfortably taking our ease by "our ain fireside."

*   *   *   *   *

A VISIT TO FINLAYSTON GLEN AND HOUSE.

TAKING the way to Finlayston by Garner's Braes, on reaching the turn of the road we descend into the green and pleasant Glen of Finlayston. This range of rising grounds which we have crossed, and from all points of which so many fine views of the Clyde, Stirlingshire, and Argyleshire are to be obtained, stretches through the parishes of Erskine, Kilmalcolm, Port-Glasgow, and Greenock, is from 300 to 500 feet in height, and is either green pasture, bare rock, or beautifully fringed with wood. As we go down through Finlayston Glen we notice two or three ash trees growing on the hill about half a mile to the right. The place is called the Gallowhill, and there the last doom of the law was carried out on the wicked caitiffs belonging to the barony of Finlayston, at that time when every laird was heritable judge on his own lands, or had the power of pot and gallows. The last doom of the law was usually carried out on hills or laws, as they are called from the circumstance, and the bodies left hanging in terrorem. Our intelligent informant, to whom we were directed as to one "who kent a' aboot the auld times," related a story to us of the end of the gallows that had long stood on this eminence, which we cannot do better than give in the vernacular: "It is a strange thing how mickle power the lairds had in auld warld times: they had the power, it seems, o' hangin' fouk at their will. Ye see yon tree up o' the hill side?" "Ay." "Weel, yon's the Gallowhill, where the gallows stood, when the lairds had the power o' life and death. A weel, there was a man that bade in a house ower by yonner, that was ta'en doun nae lang sin'; and he wanted wud for to mak' a jeest for the roof o' his house. Sae he gaes down by to the house, an' askit to see his Lordship, to ask him for the wood, for there was plenty o' trees round about then mair than there is noo. He sees his Lordship, an' tells his errand; but his Lordship didna want tae gie him nae wood, so says he, 'Ye'll get nae wood, ye'll get the gallows,' meaning to gie him a fricht. But he was a kin' o' half-witted body, and what does lie but tak' up the Earl in earnest, an' gae up neist nicht, an' taks down the gallows, and pits it into his house as a joist. That was the hin'most ane that stood there; for it was never set up again."

The House of Finlayston stands on a rising ground in the glen near the shore; and is now a plain old-fashioned building, with extensive woods and plantations around it, which occupy a great extent along the coast. A small streamlet flows pleasantly by, making a few small cascades on its way to the Firth. Finlayston was always considered a first-rate residence; but it is now of much less extent than formerly; and the railway, which passes betwixt it and the Clyde, has somewhat interfered with its quietude and amenity. It was long the chief residence of the Earls of Glencairn; a noble house; who did much good service to their country, but whose title is now extinct, and their broad lands in the possession of others.

The family of Glencairn, whose principal seat was at Kilmaurs in Cunningham, from whence they took their designation, were of great antiquity in those parts, being mentioned as early as the reign of King William, before the year 1189. But the first of this noble family who possessed the Barony of Denniestoun, was Sir William Cunningham of Kilmaurs, who married Margaret, eldest daughter and co-heiress of Sir Robert Denniestoun of that ilk, in the reign of King Robert III. Robert, his son and heir, was knighted by James the I. at his coronation. Alexander, his son and heir, was made a Baron with the title of Lord Kilmaurs; and standing loyal to King James III. in the troubles of his reign, was created Earl of Glencairn by that monarch, anno 1488. In the same year he was slain on the 14th day of June in the action at Sauchieburn in defence of his sovereign.

It were tedious to continue the history of this noble family in such a work as this: two of the Earls, who are known to all lovers of our country's letters, naturally fall to be spoken of at greater length; and do call for such a notice: but the history of the others may be found in works that treat of noble Houses, and need not to be recorded here.

On the death of John, the last Earl of Glencairn, in 1796, in accordance with the entail the estate devolved upon Robert Graham, Esq., of Gartmore, as the descendant of Lady Margaret Cunningham, eldest daughter of the 12th earl. In 1732 she was married to Nicol Graham, Esq., of Gartmore: and to her heirs the estate, but not the title, descended. A few years ago the estate was bought by Colonel Buchanan, of Drumpellier, the present proprietor.

Whilst this was the seat of the Earls of Glencairn, it was of much greater extent than it is now. At the beginning of last century, Crawfurd describes it as "The castle of Finlaystown, the seat of the Earl of Glencairn, well planted. The house is a noble and great building round a court."

We shall endeavour to give some idea of the Castle, as it was in the end of last century, when it was in possession of the Earls of Glencairn. The house took its present form at the beginning of this century. The main portion of the present house formed also the main part of the old Castle; but additions have been made to it. What was called the old wing was entirely taken down. In it was a very fine large window with gothic tracery that occupied the whole end of the wing, and commanded an extensive view. At one corner of the square stood the tall and massive round tower, probably the most ancient part of the building. In taking it down it had to be blasted with gunpowder like a rock, so thick and hard were the walls; and it was easier to break the stones in the middle than to sunder them where they had been cemented, so well did the mediaeval masons know the way to make lasting work. Let us make our way into the old Castle: here in the entrance are hanging up coats of armour, antlers of deer, &c. When we go into the great hall we look round on the pictures of the auld Earls: "I couldna get my sairin' o' lookin' at them," said our informant. "There was ane I mind fine whaur his Lordship was drawn receivin' a petition. His Lordship had on a sark wi' ruffles at the sleeves, an' ruffles at the breast o't, an' roun' about his neck; an' he had on a lang flowin' gown: ye wad hae ta'en him for a woman. They were offerin' him a petition, an' ye saw by the look on his face, that he wasna carin' about it. Whiles, I daursay, the big folk maun tak' petitions, though 'they dinna want to be fashed wi' them.'" On a pane of glass in the upper sash of a window in a bedroom in the present house, but which was the drawing-room before the present wing was built, are written with diamond pencil the words,

R. BURNS, 1768.
Under an aged oak.
AMEN.

The aged oak here referred to still stands. It is a very large spreading oak. Picnics of 150 people have been held beneath it, and three times as many could have been accommodated under its branches. At the birth of James and John, the two last earls, a larch sapling was planted; these grew and became of great size, and when cut down, about forty years ago, the workmen engaged in cutting them down remember that at their fall the roof rattled. There is a park to the east of the house called Paradise: here are some fine elm trees, under which Burns is traditionally said to have written his Lament for the Earl; but that does not agree with the words of the poem, which professes to have been written by Lugar stream. When the Earls possessed the Castle they kept up a large establishment: "There was a brew-house, and a bake-house, and a baker for their own use, and an ox was killed every week. His Lordship had thirty riding-horses, an' aucht work-horses, and rade aye wi' a great equipage. His head gardner had a hundred pounds i' the year. Na, but I wish ye could bae seen the garden. It was a big garden, and lay farrer down, nearer the Clyde. The wa's were as high as the wa's o' a house, wi' fruit trees trained up them, and vessels cut out o' sand-stone, wi' his lordship's initials carved on them, stood a' alang the tap o' the wa's. Much labour they had ta'en to mak'. They were a' ta'en to Gartmore. First the Glasgow turnpike cut off a bit o' the garden, and syne the railway took awa' anither, till there's little o't left. Mony a servant was employed about the place, an' there were houses built for them, but the place has aye been growing less an' less sin' ever I mind."

There were two ponds in the plantations near the Castle, and in the centre of one of them was an artificial island, from which to fish. There was much more plantation than there is now; much of it was cut down many years ago. Old people remember that there was a rookery in the woods. These details regarding the state of Finlayston when in the possession of the last Earls are interesting, for now the title is extinct, and the family do not possess an acre of land in the parish. At a place near the smithy of Finlayston, called Chapelhill, or Kilmalig, a few years ago, some men who were draining in a field came upon a canoe, at about three feet below the surface. It was hollowed out of a single tree, and was of considerable length and breadth.

The following story is told of the Earl and his game-keeper, Watty Macgown:- Macgown had some sheep going on the moor, who broke through the fences one day into one of his Lordship's parks. When these had been spied by his Lordship, he called Macgown in high wrath, and told him to go and "shoot those sheep." Away went the gamekeeper, and spent the afternoon in burning powder, and aiming at his flock. When evening came he returned to the house. "Well, Macgown," said his Lordship, "did you shoot any?" "Na, your Lordship," quoth the ready-witted rogue, "I tried them wi' a' kind o' powder an' ball, but the woo' was that thick the balls just stotted aff their sides." His Lordship laughed, and forgave the fault, which Macgown took good care not to repeat.

Before taking leave of Finlayston, we may mention that Wilson, in his poem of the Clyde, states that Captain

Montgomerie, author of the *Cherrie and the Slae*, stayed here for some time. We do not know his authority for saying so, but his words are as follows:--

> "But Finlayston demands the chief est lays
> A generous Muse's theme in former days,
> When soft Montgomery pour'd the rural lay;
> Whether he sung the vermeil dawn of day,
> Or in the mystic wreath, to soothe his woe,
> Twined the red cherry with the sable sloe;
> Each charming sound resistless love inspir'd,
> Soft love, resistless, every bosom fired
> Of love the waters murmur'd as they fall,
> And echo sounds of love return'd to all;
> Trembling with love, the beauteous scene impress'd
> Its amorous image on the Frith's fair breast;
> The scene ennobled by the lofty dome
> Where great Glencairn has fixed his splendid home,
> Whose breast the firm integrity inspires,
> And scorn of slavery that adorn'd his sires."

The great Glencairn here mentioned was William, the 13th Earl, a Major-General in the army, and Governor of Dumbarton Castle. He was father of James, the patron of Burns.

Finlayston may be visited from Port-Glasgow by road or rail, and from Glasgow to Langbank Station, before reaching which the line passes through the tunnel of Bishopton, one of the greatest works of the kind in the country. The line is carried through a hard ridge of solid whinstone rock for a distance of 2,300 yards. This subterranean passage took years to construct, and cost a great sum of money, the outlay for 320 tons of gunpowder, employed in the blasting operations, costing alone the sum of £12,000.

We subjoin sketches of the two Earls of this noble house most worthy of the knowledge of posterity--the "Good Earl" Alexander, friend of Knox, and supporter of the Reformation; and Earl James, the patron and benefactor of Burns.

*   *   *   *   *

ALEXANDER, THE FIFTH EARL OF GLENCAIRN,
CALLED THE "GOOD EARL."

OF the Earls of the noble house of Glencairn, two are worthy of more special notice, because they are connected with the literary history of our country. These are--Alexander, the fifth Earl, the staunch friend of Knox and the other reformers, and himself a votary of the Muses; and James, the fourteenth Earl, the patron and benefactor of Robert Burns. William, the fourth Earl, father of Alexander, befriended Wishart, on his visit to the West-land in 1544. He repaired with his followers to Ayr, where the Bishop of Glasgow was preparing to offer resistance to Wishart's preaching; and had the reformer not refused to allow it, would have taken possession of the Parish Church for him to preach in. On William's death, in the year 1547, his son, Alexander, succeeded to the estates and title. He was among the first of quality that made open profession of the Protestant religion, and showed a more than ordinary zeal in advancing the Reformation.

In the fall of the year 1555, when John Knox, coming from the North of England, where he had been preaching the Gospel, began to institute a separate communion for the Protestant Church, he visited in succession Dun, Torphichen, and Kyle, and in some of these places broke bread, after the beautiful and simple manner handed down to us in the Evangelists. He was invited by the Earl to visit

Finlayston, to preach, and dispense the Lord's Supper. The words in the Historie are:- "Before Easter [1556] the Earl of Glencarne sent for him to his place of Fynlaston, where, after sermon, he administered the Lord's Table, whereof, besides himself, were partakers, his Lady, two of his sons, and certain of his friends."

Knox was cited to be tried on the 15th May of that year, as a heretic, but his friends, who dreaded the summary proceedings that then prevailed, accompanied him in such numbers to Edinburgh that the diet was deserted. The Earl, and the Earl Marischal asked Knox to draw out his Letter to the Queen-Regent, intituled, "To the Excellent Lady Mary, Dowager, Regent of Scotland," wherein he craves for a reformation by the public authority. This was presented to her by the Earl, but failed to move her. Having read it, she handed it a few days after to the Archbishop of Glasgow, saying, with a scornful smile, "Please you, my lord, to read a pasquil."

In the year 1557, along with Lorne, Erskine, and James Stewart, the Earl wrote to Knox, at Geneva, asking him to return; and he was one of those wha signed the first covenant to defend the gospel.

When Knox landed in Scotland from France, in May of 1559, and the final struggle began, on some excesses that had been committed at Perth, the Queen Regent used great severity upon the town, whereby the heat of the people was raised to such a pitch that they broke in upon the houses of the Monks and Friars, and razed them to the ground. The Queen was so much provoked by this, that she resolved to make an example of the town. She gathered her French soldiers together, and such others as would join her, determining to put a stop to the beginnings of the Reformation: but the Reformers foresaw the hazard they stood in, and despatched letters to all their friends throughout the country, craving of them speedy help, and setting forth the nature of their demands. On these letters coming to Kyle and Cunningham, a meeting was held at the Church of Craigie, where the Earl, finding there was much diversity of opinion, spoke to this effect: "Let every man serve his conscience, I will, by God's grace, see my brethren in St. Johnston; yea, albeit never man should accompany me, yet I will go, and if it were but a pike upon my shoulder; for I had rather die with that company than live after them." "These words," continues Knox, in relating this incident, "so encouraged the rest that all agreed to go forward, as that they did so stoutly, that when the Lion Herault, in his coat of arms, commanded all men under pain of treason to return to their houses, by public sound of trumpet, in Glasgow, never man obeyed that charge, but all went forward, as we shall after hear."

By marching through deserts and mountains, this body of men, consisting of 1200 horsemen, and 1300 footmen, made such expedition that they were within six miles of the camp of the Reformers, which then lay without the town of Perth, ere they had heard of their approach. The numbers were in all about 7000 men, and the Queen Regent, by the timely arrival of this reinforcement, was afraid to engage with them: an agreement was made, oblivion promised for all that was passed, and matters of religion referred to a Parliament.

On the return of Queen Mary from France he was nominated one of the Privy Council. He was with the

Confederate Lords at Carberry hill; and, after Mary was sent
to Loch Leven, his Lordship hastened to the Chapel Royal
of Holyrood House, attended by his domestics, and broke
the images to pieces, tore down the pictures, and defaced
the ornaments of the same. "This worthy peer," to adopt the
language of Crawfurd, "who deserves to have his name
celebrated amongst the most eminent patriots of the age in
which he lived, departed this life in the year 1576," and was
succeeded by his son, William. From his poem on the Gray
Friars we may learn both the thoughts that moved him and
others like-minded of that stirring time, the turning point of
Scottish history for the last 300 years. A short poem, or
even a verse, often lets us know a man's heart and soul
better than a long story about him, which is got at second
hand. Plain is it that the old knights were not all the unlet-
tered hewers off of arms and limbs, which they are
sometimes written down to have been; and, though now
'Othello's occupation's gone,' we may well seek to vie with
them in patriotism, love of letters, and hatred of pious
frauds--

> "The knights are dust,
>   Their swords are rust,
>   Their souls are with the saints, we trust."

HIS POEM ON THE GRAY FRIARS.

The Franciscans, or Gray Friars, were an Order of much
power about the time of the Reformation, and were much
fallen away from the simplicity and good manners of the
early fathers of the Order. They were wont to be clad in a
gray cloak, with a twisted rope girded round their middle, a

cowl upon their head, and sandals on their feet; and to roam about the country, getting their living by begging, and preaching in such pulpits as were opened to them. Their mode of life put many temptations in their way, which, by the concurrent witness of the learned men and reformers of the age, they did not withstand. Erasmus and Buchanan both testify to their uselessness, and vices, and dislike of learning. Nor did the bards who wrote in our home speech say a good word of the wandering brethren. Dunbar, who was a priest himself, and had been in the ranks of the Order, when he went

"Through Picardie, and there the pepil teachit,"

asserts that, while so engaged,

"In me, God wot, was mony a wink and wile."

Sir David Lindsay has satirized their vices in his "Satire of the Three Estates." Knox's judgment of them will be seen from the extract we subjoin. True it is that in our own days Macaulay has spoken with favour of the employment of ignorant men, who have plenty of zeal, in the service of the Roman Church; and the Protestant Church seems inclined to take his advice in some cases;--and therefore we think it will be of no small profit to compare the opinions of Knox, Buchanan, and the Earl Alexander, who both knew and felt the weight of the Order, with those of our great Historian, who took his sentiments from hearsay. Knox, who has preserved the Earl's poem in his Historie, introduces it with remarks which are of much interest, as giving us his opinion of our greatest Scottish poet, the learned and excellent Buchanan. The poem itself, it will be seen, gives us in brief the sentiments of the Earl, and also clears up a point in literary history, to wit, who the Lang was who laid the Devil at Dysart, and who is sung for so doing in Buchanan's Franciscan. Knox says, speaking of James V.:

"Nane of thir terrible forewarnings [visions, &c.] could either change or mollify the heart of the indurate and licherous and avaricious tyrant, but still he does proceed from impiety till impiety. For, in the mids of thir admonitions, he caussit put hands in that notable man, Mr. George Buchanan [anno 1539], to whom, for his singular erudition and honest behaviour, was committed the chairge to instruct some of his bastard children. But, by the merciful providence of God, he escapit, albeit with great difficulty, the rage of them that sought his blood, and remains alive to this day, in the year of God 1566 years, to the glory of God, to the great honour of this nation, and to the comfort of them that delight in letters and virtue. That singular wark of David's Psalms in Latin metre and poesy, besides mony others, can witness the rare graces of God given to that man, whilk that tyrant, by instigation of the Gray Friars, and of his other flatterers, wald altogether have devorit, gif God had not providit remedy by escaping to his servant. This cruelty and persecution notwithstanding, the monsters and hypocrites, the Gray Friars, day by day came farther into contempt for not only did the learnit espy and detest their abominable hypocrisy, but also men in whom na sic graces nor gifts war thought to have been, began plainly to paint the same, forth to the people. As this rhyme, whilk here we have insertit for the same purpose, made by Alexander, Earl of Glencairn, yet alive, can witness."[1]

AN EPISTLE DIRECT FRAE THE HOLY HERMIT ALAREIT, TO HIS BRETHREN THE GRAY FRIARS.

> I Thomas, hermit in Lareit,
> Sanct Francis Order do hairtely greet,
> Beseeking you with gude intent
> To be wakerif and diligent.
> Thir Lutheranis risen of new,
> Our Order daily does persue;
> Thae smaiks does set their hail intent
> To read the English New Testament;
> And says, We have them clean deceivit,
> Therefore in haste they mon be stoppit.
> Saying that we are heretics,
> And false loud lying mastiff tykes,
> Cummerers and quellers of Christ's Kirk,
> Sweer swongeors that will not wirk,
> But idlely our living wins;
> Devouring wolves into sheep's skins,
> Our State hypocrisy they pryse,[2]
> And us blasphemis on this wise,
> Hurkling with hoods into our neck,
> With Judas' mind to jouk and beck,
> Seeking Christ's people to devore,

---

1. We are sorry to say, that on the reintroduction of some ladies of the Order, a few years ago, into Glasgow, the old spirit showed itself, "in wink and wile," by the setting agoing of a gigantic Lottery, which had to be put a stop to by the Lord Advocate.
2. Begin to perceive.

The down-thringers of Christis glore,
Professors of hypocrisy,
And doctors in idolatry,
Stout fishers with the fiendis net,
The upclosers of heaven's yett,
Cankart corruptors of the creed,
Hemlock sawers amang gude seed,
To throw in brambles that do men tyist,[1]
The high way kenning them frae Christ,
Monsters with the beastis' mark,
Doggis that never stints to bark,
Kirkmen that are to Christ unkend
A sect that Satan's self has send
Lurking in holes, like traitor todds,
Mainteners of idols and false gods,
Fantastic fules, and feignit fleechers,
To turn frae truth the very teachers;
For to declare their hail sentence
Wad mickle cumber your conscience.
To say your faith, it is sae stark,
Your cord, and lousy coat and sark,
Ye lippen may bring you to salvation,
And quite excludis Christis passion.
I dread this doctrine, and[2] it last,
Sall outher gar us wirk or fast
Therefore with speed we maun provide,
And not our profit overslide.
I shaip myself, within short while,
To curse[3] our Lady in Argyle,
And there on crafty ways to wirk,
Till that we biggit have ane kirk:

---

1. Entice
2. If.
3. Emendation, coz, or cozen.

Syne miracles mak by your advice,
They ketterils,[1] thocht[2] they had but lice,
The twa pairt to us they will bring,
But orderly to dress this thing,
A ghaist I purpose to gar gang,
By counsel of Frere Walter Lang,
Whilk sall mak certain demonstrations,
To help us in our procurations,
Your holy Order to decore.
That practic he prov'd aince before,
Betwixt Kircaldy and Kinghorn,
But limmers made thereat sic scorn,
And to his fame made sic digression,
Sinsyne he heard not the King's Confession:
Thocht at that time he come no speed,
I pray you tak gude will as deed;
And some amangst yourselves receive,
As ane worth many of the lave.
What I obtene may throw his airt,
Reason wald ye had your part.
Your Order handles no money
But other casualitie,
As beef, meat, butter, and cheese,
Or what we have, that ye please,
Send your brethren, et habete;
As now nocht ellis, but valete
Be Thomas, your brother at command,
A culrun kyth'd[3] through mony a land.

The Chapel of our Lady of Loretto, at Musselburgh, of
which the hero of this poem was hermit, or keeper, was

---

1. Caterans.
2. Though.
3. A rogue well known

often gone to by the folks of Edinburgh, when they went on pilgrimages: and writers of that age blamed the holy man, and looked on the gatherings there as fostering superstition and many other evils. Gavin Logie, a priest, when holding forth at St. Andrew's, expressed himself thus: "But now," said he, "the greediness of priests not only receive false miracles, but also they cherish and hire knaves for that purpose, that their chappels may be the better renowned, and offerings may be augmented. And thereupon are many chapels founded, as that if our Lady were mightier, and that she took more pleasure in one place than in another. But, honest men of St. Andrew's," said he, "if ye love your wives and daughters, hold them at home, or else send them in good honest company; for, if ye knew what miracles were wrought there, ye wald neither thank God nor our Lady."

We have not been able to learn anything of the doings of the Hermit in Argyle, nor what share of the spoils of the Cateran the Friars got: but the name of Lang, Confessor of King James the Fifth, is imperishably embedded in the verse of our foremost Scottish bard, Buchanan; and his adventures inlaying an evil spirit at Dysart told at length:--

> "Who had imagin'd that the rigid Scots,
>   Beneath the vertex of an icy sky,
>   Had been possess'd of spirit, eyes, or ears?
>   Yet Lang, that skilful hunter of old wives,
>   Though the grim spot and dark night aided error,
>   Could not conceal the mocks of pious fraud.
>   There was a wide uncultivated plain,
>   Where garden smiled not with various flow'r,
>   Nor field with harvest, nor a tree with boughs,
>   Scarce clad with parched shrubs the sterile sand,
>   On the lone shore the steps of cattle rare:

The neighbours call it Desert. There beneath
A rocky cave Vulcanic germs conceal
Black rugged cliffs; fires everywhere involv'd,
From veins sulphureous roll their smoky clouds,
And with a pitchy vapour reeks the soil;
And the fierce flame in caverns dark enclos'd
Cleaves spiracles on all the heaving plain,
And with huge fissures opes the yawning earth;
Hideous the place in odour, look, and state.
Oft spirits there tormented, oft complaining,
And lengthen'd voices into weeping drawn,
Lang heard, or wish'd it to be thought he heard,
And frisking devils on the barren sands
Dragging the long tracts of their winding tail:
Oft ev'n, when to the caves he fasting went,
He seem'd to inhale the infernal kitchen's smell."

Buchanan's Franciscan.

The poet thereafter goes on to tell how the priest laid the evil
spirits with an exorcism, in which he made use of holy water and
a powerful spell; how the glory of purgatory, from which the
knave, according to his own account, brought back tidings learnt
from the 'conjurit ghaists,' grew and spread till, unluckily, a
rustic, whom be had employed to help him in his pious fraud,
revealed the whole secret, and the lately waxing fame of the
King's Confessor waned away.

Henceforward therefore I admonish you
But sparely visions feign, and midnight ghosts,
And miracles, unless perhaps you say
They happen'd 'mong the far Iberians,
Or Ethiopians, or Americans,
Or under the warm heavens where the Nile
Conceals its source 'mong undiscover'd sands,
Whence none will come that can your words refute.

The Franciscan.

Thomas Douchtie, also, who is supposed to pen this epistle to his brethren, was the founder of the chapel of Loretto, where he set up his own daughter, a beautiful young woman, as an image of the Virgin Mary At this chapel, and likely enough under his superintendence, befel the unlucky splore of the herd-boy of the Sheens. This boy had the power of turning up the whites of his eyes: the nuns of Sheens, near Edinburgh, trained and bred the youth, and for seven years the young lad was known as blind. Then a miracle was announced to take place; the lad's sight was to be restored at the Chapel of our Lady of Loretto. All Edinburgh flocked to the sight: the blind lad was brought forward, mass was performed, and at the proper point in the proceedings his sight was restored. The priests were in high feather on this: but their joy was soon turned into disgrace. Among the visitors at the Shrine on occasion of the miracle had been the wife of Colville, laird of Cleish, in Fife. He got hold of the young man, and, taking him into a room, bolted the door, and, drawing his sword, declared he would have the truth out of him, or else it should be the worse for him. The lad confessed the whole affair, and offered to repeat his confession next morning at the Market Cross of Edinburgh. Accordingly, in the presence of a large crowd of witnesses, he confessed the trick, showed how it was played, avowed his contrition for the sin, and vowed amendment of life for the future. Colville and he then ran down one of the opposite closes, at the foot of which were two swift horses, saddled and bridled, on which they rode with all speed to Queensferry, and, crossing into Fife, escaped the fury of their enemies.

JAMES, THE FOURTEENTH EARL,
PATRON OF BURNS.

OF the noble Earls of the House of Glencairn, no one better merits to be kept in loving remembrance than James, the patron of our Scottish bard, Robert Burns. True is it that now-a-days there are those that say bards and men of letters are better without patrons; that aid given to a poor and struggling poet would be better withheld; and that the praise the bard gives in return for the pudding is fulsome, naught, and fleeching. This we take the leave to doubt: a lord, or wealthy merchant, who has wit enough to pick out a truly good poet or writer of merit, and large-hearted enough to spend money for him, or see to his welfare otherwise, is a higher kind of man than he who spends his fortune on the pleasing of himself alone, or even the welfare of his kith and kin. It is not the having of a patron that is a bad thing; but the having of a foolish patron. Unluckily now-a-days, however, the old way, ennobling alike to giver and receiver, is out of date. The, new way, to be sure, gives us a kind of poetry, and a kind of literature: but we doubt, after all, whether the old was not better. Whoever wills to be a patron of the right sort gives not mere sympathy-that is of no use to the clan of bards, who have feeling and to spare of their own-but sees to what they are oftentimes ill fitted to do, to wit, getting their pockets lined with gold. He also reads, and judges, the works of the receiver of his care. Above all, he takes care not to put off the giving of his favour till the poet is dead; and then begin to feast in his honour, and to his own glory, as often happens. Who does not wish that Tannahill had had a patron? Who, that Burns had had a few more like the noble Earl of Glencairn.

James, the fourteenth Earl of Glencairn, was born in June, 1749, and succeeded his father in 1775, being then abroad on a tour through Norway, Lapland, and Sweden. He was captain of a company of the West Fencible Regiment, 1778; was chosen one of the sixteen representatives of the Scottish Peerage at the general election, 1780, and supported Fox's India Bill, 1783. He disposed of his ancient family estate of Kilmaurs to the Marchioness of Titchfield, 1786; sailed for Lisbon, 1790; and dying unmarried soon after landing from thence, at Falmouth, on the 30th of January, 1791, in the 42nd year of his age, was buried in the chancel of the church there.

His brother John, the last Earl, was first an officer in the Fourteenth Regiment of Dragoons, and afterwards took orders in the Church of England; and died at Coats, near Edinburgh, 24th September, 1796, in the 47th year of his age, and is buried at St. Cuthbert's, where is a monument thus inscribed: "The Right Honourable and Right Reverend John, Earl of Glencairn, was interred here the 29th September, 1796 aged 46 years." On his death the estate of Finlayston (but not the title of Glencairn) devolved on Robert Graham, Esq. of Gartmore.

Burns's works and merits were first brought under the notice of the Earl James by Mr. Alexander Dalzell, factor at Finlayston. Some of his poems were sent for the perusal of his Lordship, and his sister, Lady Elizabeth Cunningham, and the other members of his family. On Burns's visit to Edinburgh, in the year 1786, he was introduced to his Lordship, and by him to the circle in which he moved, and to Creech, the publisher of the second edition of his poems. In a letter to John Ballantine, Esq., banker, Ayr, of date 16th Dec., 1786, the poet says: "By his interest (the Earl's) it is passed in the ' Caledonian Hunt,' and entered in their books, that they are to take each a copy of the second edition, for which they are to pay one guinea. I have been introduced to a good many of the noblesse, but my avowed patrons and patronesses are--the Duchess of Gordon; the Countess of Glencairn, with my Lord, and Lady Betty; the Dean of Faculty, Sir John Whiteford."

This second edition of his poems brought Burns in several hundred pounds, and gained him almost all the gain he ever made by his pen. He afterwards asked the Earl's interest for a place in the excise; we do not know with what result. But the gratitude of the poet to his Lordship was most fervent; and he always looked on him as the kindest benefactor he had ever had. In a letter to Mr. Alexander Dalzell, above mentioned, written from Ellisland on the 19th of March, he expresses his poignant sorrow at the loss of his friend and patron: "God knows what I have suffered at the loss of my best friend, my first and dearest patron and benefactor; the man to whom I owe all that I am and have! I am gone into mourning for him, and with more sincerity of grief than I fear some will who, by nature's ties, ought to feel on the occasion."

And in another to Lady Elizabeth Cuningham, the sister of the late Earl, he says: "Nor shall my gratitude perish with me! If among my children I have a son that has a heart, he

shall hand it down to his child as a family honour and a
family debt, that my dearest existence I owe to the house of
Glencairn."

Burns's connection with this noble and gifted family is
one of the most pleasant things in his chequered life. One of
his sons he named James Glencairn Burns, after his loved
patron. One cannot but think that, had the Earl been longer
spared, the misfortunes of the bard might have been
lessened, or altogether warded of his much admired Lament
for this friend of letters, a few verses are here sub-joined.

LAMENT FOR JAMES, EARL OF GLENCAIRN.

The wind blew hollow frae the hills,
By fits the sun's departing beam
Look'd on the fading yellow woods
That wald o'er Lugar's winding stream.

Beneath a craigy steep a bard,
Laden with years and meikle pain,
In loud lament bewailed his lord,
Whom death had all untimely slain.

And last (the sum of a' my griefs!)
My noble master lies in clay;
The flow'r amang our barons bold,
His country's pride! his country's stay!

In weary being now I pine,
For a' the life of life is dead,
And hope has left my aged ken,
On forward wing for ever fled.

In poverty's low barren vale

Thick mists obscure involv'd me round,
Though oft I turn'd to wistful eye,
No ray of fame was to be found

Thou found'st me like the morning sun,
That melts the fogs in limpid air,
The friendless bard and rustic song
Became alike thy fostering care.

The bride-groom may forget the bride,
Was made his wedded wife yestreen;
The monarch may forget the crown,
That on his head an hour has been;

The mother may forget the child,
That smiles sae sweetly on her knee;
But I'll remember thee, Glencairn,
An' a' that thou hast done for me.

*   *   *   *   *

FINLAYSTONE COUNTRY ESTATE,
BY
CHRIS MORRISON.

IF *Kilmalcolm*, becoming *Kilmacolm*, lost a letter from the time of Alexander Gibb, then *Finlayston*, becoming *Finlaystone*, gained one. There have been a number of owners of Finlaystone House and estate since the author penned those last few chapters.

Pages describing the history of Finlaystone through the centuries can be read on-line at the estate's web-site at http://www.finlaystone.co.uk.

Briefly, Finlaystone fell into the hands of the Grahams of Gartmore for a period. Gamblers and others aside, one of the best known of this family is Robert Bontine Cunninghame-Graham, a great and true Scot in every way. It is interesting to note that "Don Roberto," as our intrepid Scot was affectionately known, is buried on the island of Inchmahome, the largest of three islands, on the Lake of Menteith, Stirlingshire. The Canon of Inchmahome in 1548 was Alexander Scott whose poem "of may" we have reprinted in a later chapter. He was organist at the Augustinian Priory of Inchmahome. The dulcet notes of a Renaissance piece drifting over the Lake of Menteith on a May morning must have been a wonderful concert to witness.

In 1863 Sir David Carrick-Buchanan became owner of Finlaystone and in 1897 George Jardine Kidston (1835-

1909) acquired it. He employed the celebrated architect J. J. Burnet to make some tasteful changes to the house. Through the Kidston family Finlaystone came into the hands of the MacMillan family; the current owners.

The gardens and woodlands of Finlaystone estate are truly delightful and attract many visitors each year. There is a charge for admission. The range of habitats and wildlife are carefully managed and each time I visit I always see something new, whether it be an insect, a fungi, a bird or animal or wild flower. Considering that there is something like 140 acres of woodland with some trees estimated to be 300-400 years old this is no small wonder.

International Dawn Chorus Day falls on the first Sunday of May each year. It would be precious if an event was organised at Finlaystone on a dewy May morn. Of all the places in Renfrewshire to hear a concert of such sweetness, Finlaystone has to be one of the best.

Share the secret.

*   *   *   *   *

A VISIT TO BADRENEY, THE BOGLE STANE, NEWARK CASTLE, PORT-GLASGOW, AND DEVOL'S GLEN.

WE set out in the morning after breakfast, to pay a visit to "The Port," as Port-Glasgow is called in the neighbourhood, by way of eminence. A fine morning it is! A blue sky overhead, flecked only with a few light-clouds; and the delightsome sunshine bathing field and farm, vale and hill, with its clear radiance--

> "A day so pure, so calm, so bright,
> The bridal of the earth and sky."

The lark is up betimes, and is discoursing sweet melody. Yonder from the marsh rises the heron, and, soaring aloft, slowly disappears in the blue sky. In those boggy marshes, were it not too late in the season, we might get by wading the beautiful flower of the bog bean. But we see none at present, nor are we in a mood to wade for them. On that wooded height to our left there is said to be a Roman Lamp as the Romans certainly had a station at Paisley, it is likely they would have an outlying camp hereabout. Some years ago two vases were found there; one of them was broken by the inadvertence of a workman; the other was preserved, and is now in the possession of William Brown, Esq., M.D. The road now passes through a dreary and moorland tract, relieved only by a few farms, and separating Kilmalcolm from the outer world, according to the old saying, "Out of the world and into Kilmalcolm."

We turn aside from the highway in order to pay a brief visit to Badreney, a tall and deserted-looking building, standing on the top of the hill about a mile to the south-east of Port-Glasgow. For the latter years of the last century, and the early years of the present, this house was the abode of Alexander Dalzell, Esq., factor for the Earls of Glencairn and other gentlemen. He was a correspondent of Robert Burns, and to him is due the credit of first calling the attention of his Lordship, and of the family, to the merits of the Ayrshire ploughman. In this way his name becomes worthy of remembrance, as that of one who had the chance of doing a good deed, and who did it. He is described as having been in person tall and gaunt, and he lived single all his life. The school-boys of Kilmalcolm, when returning from the Port-Glasgow schools, were wont to feel frightened in the mirky gloamin' as they left the huge Bogle Stone behind and entered on the moors, lest they should meet Dalzell by the way; for a rumour ran that he had dealings wi' the deil. Dalzell had a curious way of speaking about his heir. He said, "he was to be a minister body; he did not know if he were good for anything or not." Latterly Mr. Dalzell held a good many farms on the Finlayston estate, in grassum. In this way the proprietor was put into the possession of a round sum of ready money; Dalzell repaid himself out of the rents, and at his death the farms reverted to the estate. Of his sharp business habits we were told the following story:--

Our informant, then a boy of four or five years of age, was present in the Castle of Finlayston with his father, when the latter went to settle an account of some amount which he was due to the factor. He laid down the money on the table. Dalzell glanced over it, counted it, and, quoth he," You're due me a ha'penny; oh, but never mind!" Such a remark casts a flood of light on the character of this friend of our Scottish bard, and shows him as the shrewd, sharp man of business.

We get from here diversified prospects of the mountains of Argyle, of Ben Lomond, and the peaks of the Perthshire mountains, and nearer at hand Dumbartonshire, with the opposite coast, from Kilpatrick down to Roseneath. We now begin to bethink ourselves that we are in a region where of old times scenes and legends of another world were believed in. Here, growing in a turnip field, we see the mugwort plant, a tall spare herb, which in old world stories was held a specific for a wasting, or consumption. Mr. Robert Chambers relates that a visitant once appeared from the deep to sing the mystic virtues of this herb. As the funeral of a young woman, who had died of consumption, was passing along the high road, on the shore of the Firth of Clyde above Port-Glasgow, says he, a mermaiden raised her head from the waves, and, in slow admonitory tones, addressed the bearers these words:

> "If they wad drink nettles in March,
> An' eat muggons in May,
> Sae mony braw maidens
> Wadna gang to the clay."

And, in consequence of this, muggons, or mugwort, and nettle kail, were held to be a specific in this fatal ailment. After the example of the eating of rats and horses and dogs in the siege of Paris, we would be chary of saying that nettle kail, or muggin broo', was not good for the health: but we would back the fresh air of Kilmalcolm, and the sweet milk from the dairies, that supply Port-Glasgow and Greenock with their produce, to effect a cure sooner than either mugwort or nettle. But here we are at "Rest and be Thankfu'" and the Bogle Stane, a large quadrangular block of whin eight or nine feet high, that stands in the corner o^, a field close by the wayside. It has a grassy top, to which we mount, and find it could accommodate half-a-score of persons on it. This far-famed stone stands on the farm of Laigh Auchinleck, and was once larger than it is now, and thereby hangs a tale. This large block was famed for a bogle, or sort of impish sprite, that used to haunt it in days of yore. When folks had been visiting the Port, as Burns says--

> "When we sit bousing at the nappy,
> And getting fou' and unto happy,
> We think na on the lang Scots miles,
> The mosses, waters, slaps, and stiles,
> That lie between us and our hame."

When the delinquent had clomb up the brae, and had got out of sight of the lights of the town, and was just entering on the wild and dreary moor that separates Kilmalcolm from the outer world, the Bogle was frequently seen about this stone, and sent the belated worthy onward at accelerated speed, while he fancied he heard a something following at his heels. The good wives of Kilmalcolm used to say that, whether it were a ghaist or a deil, it was a god-send to the kintra, for it sent home Kilmalcolm folks at a richt like time o' nicht.

It came to pass, however, some time not yet very remote, that a clergyman, whether taking a dislike at vexatious folks holding picnics, junketings, and frolics upon the Stone, or being in want of whin to build his dykes, or wishing to abolish what he regarded as a relic of superstition, we know not, but he resolved to have the stane destroyed. Accordingly, much of it was blasted; some built into dykes, and some used otherwise. "Mony a guid curling-stane cam oot o't," as we were told, "for, ye see, it polishes weel." But this deed of his reverence roused a nest of hornets about his ears; the act was denounced, and the vandalism of it shown up. Ultimately, on a new proprietor coming into possession, the pieces were re-united, and now the Bogle Stane looks "amaist as guid as new." A local poet wrote the following verses on the occasion, which were at one time inscribed on the side of the stone, but are now rubbed off:

> "Ye weary travellers passing by,
>   Rest and be thankfu' here,
>   And should your lips be parch'd and dry,
>   Drink of my waters clear.
>
> I am that far-famed Bogle Stane,
>   By worldly priest abhorr'd,
>   But now I am myself again,
>   By Auchinleck restored."

Leaving "Rest and be Thankfu'," after taking a drink of the waters, we go down the brae by Clune-brae Toll, stopping every now and then to have a view of the scenery, which is here seen to great advantage. Away to the eastward the Clyde is seen rolling downwards by Bowling, with the Kilpatrick hills, clad with shaggy woods on their sides; and the Rock of Dumbarton looming darkly against them. The eye ranges along the Cardross shore, with the headland of Ardmore stretching out into the Firth; and the snowy villas of Helensburgh and Row rising upon the water side. Westward lie Port-Glasgow and Greenock, with many stately ships lying at the Tail of the Bank, waiting for the tide to ascend the river. Beyond are the Gareloch and Loch Long, and the rugged masses of the Argyleshire mountains behind, with the shadows of lofty clouds flecking their expanse. But we now descend the brae, noting that the slope is thickly studded with pleasant houses, and enter Port-Glasgow; and first make our way to the old Castle of Newark.

NEWARK CASTLE.

Stands a little to the east of the town, on a slightly raised terrace close to the Firth, of which it commands a fine prospect both up and down, and of the shore of Dumbarton that lies over against it. As we approach the ancient pile, we are reminded of the busy modern world of trade by hearing the clang of the hammers rivetting bolts in the iron-ship building yards, one of which is set down on either side of the Castle. Making our way into the court through an arched doorway, we perceive that the edifice consists of a keep, of the beginning of the fifteenth century, with additions of a lower period, but rich in carved devices and ciphers, and is a remarkable specimen of the Scotch manor-house of the date marked by the inscription over the door, partially defaced: "The blessingis of God be herein. 1597." The keep, or oldest part of the building, stands at the south-east corner, and is now roofless. The windows are many of them carved,

and the workmanship still well defined; and over several of
them are the letters P. M. (Patrick Maxwell), the initials of
the baronet by whom the more modern part of the edifice
was reared. Above one of the windows are the figures 1599.
The Castle consists of three rectangular compartments: the
principal face of the building looks towards the river, and is
ornamented with corbelled turrets at the corners, and one
projecting from the central wall. The building is inhabited
by some families of work people. We notice a curious round
building, standing a little apart, which we recognised as a
dove-house, or columbarium, which is often found in the
neighbourhood of old castles.

Newark Castle was the principal messuage of the Barony
of Denniestoun-Maxwell, which, with divers other lands,
came to Sir Robert Maxwell of Calderwood, a younger son
of the family of Nether-Pollock, in right of Elizabeth, his
wife, second daughter and one of the co-heiresses of Sir
Robert Dennistoun of that ilk, about the middle of the
fifteenth century.The barony of Dennistoun, which
stretched from the Clyde to the Gryfe, was then divided into
two, one the aforesaid, and the other Dennistoun-Cunning-
ham. None of the owners of Newark call for particular
remark. About the beginning of last century George
Maxwell sold his patrimony to Mr. William Cochrane, of
Kilmaronock. Afterwards the castle and barony passed into
the possession of Sir James Hamilton of Rosehaugh, and
from his family by succession to Lord Belhaven, who in
turn sold it to Mr. Farquhar, of London, from whom, by
inheritance, it came into the possession of Sir Michael Shaw
Stewart, Bart., the present proprietor. The castle ceased to
be inhabited by its owners at an early period of the last

century; and since then it is being allowed to fall gradually into decay: but the situation is so good that in old times it must have formed a delightful residence, though in our days the neighbourhood of a busy and bustling sea-port town robs it of the quietude and repose which are requisite for gentlemen's seats.

Leaving this massive pile with regret, we proceed to perambulate the streets and quays of Port Glasgow, and to see the various objects of interest which it presents to tourists; but instead of enumerating them one by one, as we chanced to come upon them, it will be better to give a general description of the town, whereby visitors will learn what is most worthy of being known.

PORT-GLASGOW.

The earliest notice of the burgh and barony of Newark, which is now included in Port-Glasgow, occurs in a report of Thomas Tucker, one of Cromwell's officers of excise, to the Commissioners of Appeals, in the year 1656 [* Macdonald's Days at the Coast.] He says: "The number of ports in this district are, (1st) Newarke, a small place where there are (besides the laird's house of the place), some four or five houses, but before them a prettye good roade, where all the vessels doe ride, unlaide, and send their geodes up the river to Glasgow in small boates. At this place there is a wayter constantly attending." But about this time the merchants of Glasgow resolved to construct a harbour at the mouth of the river, to accommodate their shipping; for the navigation of the Clyde was then impeded above Dumbarton by shallows and islands, so that only vessels of a few tons burthen could ascend to the Broomielaw. Accordingly, they pitched upon

Dumbarton as the most suitable locality, and applied to the Town Council for leave to erect the necessary works. A meeting of the Council was accordingly held, when it was resolved to refuse the grant, on the ground that "the influx of mariners would tend to raise the prices of butter and eggs to the inhabitants." A similar application at Troon was repulsed on the same grounds. In these circumstances, Sir Patrick Maxwell of Newark offered to feu to the Magistrates of Glasgow about fourteen acres of land; and, in the year 1668, they erected a harbour for the accommodation of their shipping. As the navigable part of the Firth, called the Channel, lies here close along the shore, and was then about 200 yards broad, and everywhere so deep that at high water the largest vessels that navigated the Clyde could be moored in the harbour without discharging their cargoes, it was a very fit place for that purpose. It was erected by King Charles II. into the Burgh of Barony of Port-Glasgow (formerly called Devol's Glen). In process of time the burgh extended, and included the neighbouring village of Newark within its bounds. In the year 1695, the Burgh of Barony of Port-Glasgow, and the Bay of Newark, and a narrow strip of hilly land extending about a mile backward up the country, were disjoined from the parish of Kilmalcolm, and erected into a distinct parish, to which the name of New Port-Glasgow, or Port-Glasgow, was given. In 1710 it was made the seat of the Custom Office for the precinct of Clyde; and the merchants of Glasgow were required to discharge their goods here. After the deepening of the river, and the substitution of the Broomielaw as the proper sea-port of Glasgow, the relative importance of Port-Glasgow decreased; but it still retains a good share of trade. In 1760 the first dry or graving dock in Scotland was built here: the extreme length of it, from the gates to the head of the dock on the floor, was 253 feet; it admitted of one vessel of 500 tons, or of two of 300 or 400 at a time. But far greater interest attaches to Port-Glasgow, inasmuch as the first successful steamboat ever built in Britain was constructed here. Mr. Henry Bell, of Helensburgh, after trying in vain to enlist the British Government of the day in his schemes of steamboat navigation, though Lord Nelson expressed his opinion that Mr. Bell ought to be encouraged, sent plans of his schemes to various European, and to the American, Governments. On the part of the latter, Mr. Fulton was appointed to correspond with Bell, with whom he also held intercourse on a visit to this country. Fulton built the first successful steamboat on the Hudson in the year 1807. In 1812 Bell was able to raise the means to build the Comet, the first steamboat to ply in European waters. She was built for him by Mr. Henry Wood, of Port-Glasgow, and plied first between Glasgow and Greenock. Afterwards Mr. Bell wished to lengthen her; but, as he thought the price asked by Mr. Wood too high, he had her beached at Helensburgh, and altered under his own direction. The timber he used was fir, and when she was wrecked on the Dorus More, she parted at the point of junction, which seems to indicate that the workmanship had not been good. Mr. William Thomson, civil engineer, in a letter to Mr. Edward Morris, the true friend and biographer of Bell, gives the following account of the destruction of the little Comet, the prototype of the many stately steam-vessels that now throng the waters of the Clyde, bound for the most distant lands and seas. He says:

"In October, 1820, when on her passage from Fort William to Glasgow, in which Mr. Bell had accompanied her to make arrangements with subscribers about a new and more powerful boat for the ensuing season, the weather being then very unfavourable for a boat of such limited power as the old Comet was; yet making a favourable passage till entering the Dorus More, and rounding the point-head of Craignish, she was met by a strong easterly wind, from which she had been previously comparatively sheltered, by which, and a rapid current which prevails there, her head was forced about towards the land, and her bow run ashore between the rocks, which fortunately admitted Mr. Bell and his companions to get ashore. The boat soon after parting in two, the after-part floated towards the gulf of Corrywreckain, and the bow rested where the accident occurred, from which part of the machinery was afterwards recovered."

Port-Glasgow had the advantage from the first of being laid off according to a regular plan, and with more consideration as to the width of the streets than has been paid in the neighbouring town of Greenock. The houses too are constructed with a considerable degree of uniformity, and some of them are quaint and handsome, with ancient-looking windows and peaked gables. The town nestles, as it were, round the quays and docks which project into the river, and afford a capital prospect of the Firth both upwards and downwards. It looks well, whether seen from the steamer or from the land, and maintains a comparatively healthy condition. Some of the public buildings are really handsome, in particular the Town-house, with massive portico and spire, built from the designs of David Hamilton,

Esq., architect in Glasgow. There are churches belonging to the various denominations. The heights, which rise to the south of the town to the height of 600 or 700 feet, are to a considerable distance up variegated with fields, orchards, trees, elegant villas, and gardens with pleasant walks winding among them. These residences of the merchants and manufacturers, which also are planted farther up the coast side, acid greatly to the beauty of the scenery.

The principal trade of Port-Glasgow is the timber trade. In the end of the year the vessels arrive from Quebec loaded with cargoes of Canadian pine, which are deposited in the many wood-ponds which, formed of upright stabs of wood, are seen fringing the coast both up and down. Iron ship-building is also carried on to a large extent, as also is sugar-refining, and the manufacture of canvas, and rope-making. Two steamers plying between Glasgow and Rothesay call in summer, and there is constant railway communication with Greenock, Paisley, and Glasgow. The population of the town has been increasing rapidly of late, and is now about 10,000.

In the world of letters Port-Glasgow has the honour of giving birth to Daniel Macphail, the author of "Blythe, blythe around the nappy," and other songs of worth. He lived most of his life, however, in Glasgow, where he died in poverty, the wonted lot of poets, about the year 1833. He was a wright to his trade. We give a few verses from his Days o' Lang-syne.

0 happy, happy were the days o' auld langsyne,
The hamely sweets, the social joys o' auld langsyne,
When ilka ane wi' friendly glow and cordial heart wad join,

To pledge wi' friendship leal and true the days o' langsyne.

How sweet the fond endearing charms o' auld langsyne,
Wi' Jeanie in my youthfu' arms, in days o' langsyne,
In rapture prest her throbbing breast wi' glowing love to mine,
Thae happy hours flew o'er wi' bliss in days o' langsyne.

Amang our native woods and braes how pleasant the time,
To pu' for her I lo'ed sae clear the primrose in its prime:
Then fairer bloom'd ilk bonnie flow'r, mair sweet the birds did sing,
When wi' the lass I dearly lo'ed, in days o' langsyne
.
Nae mair amang our bonnie glens we'll garlands entwine,
Nor pu' the wild-flower by the burn, to husk my lassie fine;
Nae mair upon yon sunny knowe we'll mark the sun decline,
Nor tell the tender tales that pleased in days o' langsyne.

DEVOL'S GLEN.

Is a wild and rugged ravine that lies a little to the westward
of the town, and thither after a rest and refreshment we bend
our course. Crawfurd informs us that the place on which
Port-Glasgow was built, was formerly called Devol's glen;
that would be in old time when the heath and moor came
down to the sea., and the chief occupation of the few inhabitants was the herring fishing in the Clyde, to which they
went, about the time of the Restoration, three times a year,
which times were called the Drave; and from Greenock,
Crawfordsdike, Gourock, and Inverkip the greatest number
of boats used to go out. What a different scene does the
Firth present, as we stop to look back upon it today; studded
as it is with the largest steamers, and ships hastening up to
Glasgow, or out to all parts of the world, and Greenock and
Newark, no longer little fishing hamlets, but almost joined

into one city, and filling the space betwixt the hills and the Firth. But we ascend the ravine and come first to the Lady's Linn, a pretty little cascade about twenty feet in height, over which the streamlet descends. We ascend by the western side of the Glen, and cross the Railway from Greenock, which here spans the hollow in a viaduct of nine arches. As we look up at the slender pillars rising out of the sloping brae, and supporting the mass above, along which a heavy train is thundering, we wonder how they do not slip down altogether, and precipitate the structure to the bottom of the defile. But no; engineering skill is too sure an art to permit anything of the sort. The Railway that winds up the vale of Kilmalcolm here descends a very steep gradient from the top of the ridge above the Bogle Stane, along the face of the brae above Port-Glasgow down to Greenock, and affords to the passengers a surprising glimpse of the beautiful scenery of the Firth by day, and one almost as striking of swiftly fleeting lamps and lights by night. As we ascend farther we are delighted with the various tints and hues which give variety to the well-wooded sides of the glen, from the dark green of the fir, to the light green of the rowan tree, whose berries hang in clusters on the boughs that wave over the crags. The songsters of the grove are silent; the rivulet trickles with a soft murmur at the bottom of the dell; and the mellow sunshine floods with light the woods and the heath. We recall the words of the poet,

> Ho, young men! who, the dark and slothful shades
> Scorning, and city's noise, and tavern black,
> Dares climb into the airy tracts of woods,
> And near the founts where revel lands of Nymphs,
> And meadows aye renew'd with purple youth?

A little farther up we dive into the glen to visit the Wallace leap, a rugged precipitous crag which rises sheer from the bottom of the stream, and over the top of which that renowned hero is said by tradition to have urged his steed, and to have alighted unscathed on the opposite side. A little time ago a greyhound in pursuit of a fox went over the same dizzy cliff, but was not so fortunate, for he was found dashed to pieces at the bottom. The stream here leaps over another higher linn; and the whole scene is one very romantic, and fitted to delight the painter and the poet. On reaching the top of the ridge on the edge of the moor, which, according to the saying common' in Greenock and Port-Glasgow, "out of the world and into Kilmalcolm," separates that village and valley from all the world, we are greeted with a prospect of the utmost beauty and magnificence. From all parts of this ridge the view is much admired; but the point we have now reached is confessedly the finest. To the eastward the scene is magnificent: the Clyde rolling downwards by Dunglass, Dumbuck, and the woody steeps of the Kilpatrick hills, skirted on the one side by the richly wooded heights of Broadfield and Finlayston, and on the other by the Dumbartonshire coast, while the rocky crag of Dumbarton rises from the waves, and seems the natural guardian of the Firth. Opposite is the diversified coast of Cardross, with heathy fells beyond, and in the distance the rocky peak of Benlomond over-topping the scene. Westward on the opposite coast, are the snowy villas of Helensburgh, set down amid wide space, which gives it the appearance of a large city, the villas and woods of Row, the Gareloch, Roseneath, Kilcreggan, Lochlong, and Kilmun, are successive points of beauty: while the dark rugged lofty

masses of the Argyleshire hills form a magnificent amphi-
theatre in the background. On this side are the steeples,
chimneys, and crowded abodes of Greenock and Gourock.
The basin of the Firth is dotted with steamers, ships, and
boats, on their various errands of pleasure or usefulness: the
whole forming one of the fairest scenes that can delight the
eye.

A road leads from this point through the moors to
Kilmalcolm by the vale of the Gryfe; another track goes
along the top of the ridge to Rest and be Thankful, which
affords many diversified prospects of the Coast. As for us
we prefer to hold down to Greenock, and take, the last train
for Kilmalcolm.

THE VISION OF AULD DUNROD AT THE BOGLE STANE.

> "In Innerkyp the witches ride thick,
> And in Dunrod they dwell;
> But the grittest loon amang them a'
> Is auld Dunrod[1] himsel."
>> *Old Rhyme.*

> Auld Dunrod was a warlock gude,
> Wha wonned by the Clyde;
> He sleepit on the Bogle Stane,
> And there this vision spied.

> He lookit owr the loch o' Clyde,

---

1. Dunrod belonged to a family of the name of Lindsay. As
   Alexander Lindsay, the last laird of Dunrod of the name, sold
   the estate in 1619, Chambers thinks this old rhyme as old at
   least as that date.

A sicht o' glamourie,
For forests wide o' firren trees
Cam doun close to the sea.

An' whiles in openings o' the wud
A clan's abode he saw,
A' set about wi' palisades,
That stood up in a raw.

The hovels were o' wattles made,
An' were chokefu' o' reek;
Lasses were liltin' at the quern,
A' browned wi' the smeek.

But what is you at Kempock point?
Canoes glide, twa or three,
A' hew'd wi' stonen axe, and fire,
Out of a gude fir tree.

An' in them naked savages,
He counted dozens twa,
Wi' wild beasts scor'd upon their skins,
The queerest ere he saw.

Good blades had they, blunt at the end,
That were baith sharp an' sheen,
An' spears that rattled when they flew,
An' bows an' arrows keen.

They paidled up an' down the firth,
Ilk man his own canoe;
For naething then but boats o' tree
Were on Clyde's waters blue.

When to! owr Gourock-point he saw
A sicht o' meikle pride;

There were twenty Roman ships an' three
Cam rowin' up the Clyde.

Fill'd the sails were wi' the wind,
The oarsmen plied the oar; -
An' tenty the mid-channel kept,
An' shunn'd the banky shore.

A' roundabout the galley's sides
The shields hung-in a raw;
The mariners wi' wonder gazed
On the heich hills they saw.

An' some row'd up, an' farrer up,
Until Dunglass they gain,
Aboon the great Rock of the Clyde,
That tow'rs above the plain.

There on the shore the camp was built,
For there the legions lay;
An' Julius[1] the rampart rear'd
To keep the clans at bay.

Then mariners and soldiers,
They mingled on the shore;
These told of mountains, those of seas
And isles ne'er seen before.

Then camp an' galleys vanished

---

1. Julius Agricola, who invaded North Albion, A.D. 81. The
   German seamen of a galley stationed on the West Coast muti-
   nied, seized the ship, and, carrying her round the north of
   Albion, reached the German coast, where they spread abroad
   flaming accounts of the islands, and nations they had seen.

Before that warlock's e'en;
An' lo! before his wond'ring gaze
Appears a peaceful scene.

Still as of yore the sea-loch fills
The hollow of the hills;
Still ebbeth when the ocean ebbs,
And when that flows, it fills.

Still branching lochs afar ascend
Among the mountains high;
An' still that Rock of Clyde stands fast,
While rolls the river by.

But changed the scene from what it was
Two thousand years ago;
Nor tree-canoe the river bears,
Nor presence of a foe.

But iron vessels to and fro
On varied pathways glide;
Some driv'n by wind, an' some by steam,
Right gallantly they ride.

For Broomielaw these hold their course,
Ascending 'gainst the stream;
For Erin, or the Hudson those,
Or the Wrest Highlands steam.

The mariner, as up he's tugg'd
The river's banks alang,
Of shipwrights building iron ships
He hears the hammers clang.

The warlock sees the glassy firth

A' gay wi' sails an' boats,
Yachts, schooners, tugs, brigs, an' ships,
A' kind o' thing that floats

He sees the Gareloch windin' up,
Wi' villas on its side;
An' Helensburgh's snawy cots
Uprising frae the tide.

Thy flow'ry fields, O Cardross fair,
Appear'd before his e'en;
Dumbarton's town, Dumbarton's Rock,
Beside the waves are seen.

Kilpatrick's hills, wi' rugged braes,
A glimpse of Leven-side;
An' far awa Ben Lomond's peaks,
With streaks of snow, are spied.

There thronging Greenock he beheld,
Port-Glasgow on the brae;
An' high Argyle's magnificence
Of mountains far away.

A fairy picture sure did then
Before that wizard shine
When hark! an engine shakes the earth,
And thunders clown the line.

The puffing smoke, the flying wheels,
An' the air-shaking sound,
Awakened that wizard hoar
Out of his seer's stound.

The ferlies which he saw that day
He had nae words to say

He wauken'd, an' he only heard
Winds whistlin' on the brae,

An' the whaups pipin' on the bent,
An' beetles' drowsy drone,
An' mair-cocks wi' their bid-bid-birr,
'Upon the moorlands lone.

Syne he to Kilmalcolm's sweet vale
Has ta'en his homeward way;
But never till he de'ed forgat
The ferlies o' that day.

*   *   *   *   *

VISIT TO BRIDGE OF WEIR AND KILBARCHAN,

WE must not forget to pay a visit to Kilbarchan by way of Bridge of Weir. We may go to the latter by rail, or by driving, or on Shank's naigie. Going down the valley we mark Duchal House, in the hollow on our right, surrounded with plantations. On coming near Bridge of Weir we see on our left a hillock of some size called Castle Gryfe, which is said to have been a moot-hill, or meeting hill in auld world days; but never to have been graced with a castle as the name might lead one to think. Bridge of Weir is a thriving manufacturing place, sometimes celebrated by admirers as being a suburb of Glasgow. It must be owned it has at least two of the marks of the big city, thriving industry and plenty of smoke. On the rising grounds to the south stand the ruins of Ranfurly Castle, which was long in the possession of a family of Knoxes: Knox himself, the Scottish reformer, was a cadet of this house, though he was born at Haddington in East Lothian. There is little of the old pile remaining, and that is fast crumbling down. Near the ruin is an earthen mound, supposed to have been a moot hill, from which a good view is obtained.

But Kilbarchan has the most claims on our attention. In a niche in the steeple of the church stands a statue of Habbie Simson, the renowned Piper of Kilbarchan, whose name occurs in Maggie Lauder, in Ramsay's works, and Beattie's, and who seems to have been a rare good fellow in his day.

He is represented here with his cheeks puffed out with wind, and blowing away with might and main. We need say nothing more of Habbie, as we give at the end of this chapter the Epitaph written on him by Robert Sempill, of Beltrees, which is the source of all his fame. The poem we may state first appeared in James Watson's Collection of Scotch Poems, Part I., 1706.

Robert Sempill, the author, was served heir of his father, October 12, 1625, in the lands of Yochar, Blavarthill, Kingsmedow, &c. He was likely born in 1595, his parents having been married in 1594. He was educated at Glasgow College; married Mary, daughter of Sir Thomas Lyon of Auldbar, in Angus; and was an officer in the Royalist army during the troubles of the Civil War. He seems not to have flourished greatly in wealth, for on the 10th March, 1649, R. Sempill and his spouse, Dame Marie Lyoune, contract a wadset disponing "all and haille thaire twa pairte of the fyve merk land of Auchinlodmont, with houses, zairds, &c., by and within the parochin of Paisley, to Capitaine Livetennent George Montgomerie, for £3000." The date of his death is unknown, but he must have been dead before 28th June, 1669, as on that date his son, Francis Sempill of Beltrees, is mentioned as possessor of the family estate. The poem itself is called by Ramsay "Standart Habbie," in all likelihood referring to the measure, of which it is the first, or one of the first, specimens--a measure since used with fine effect by Burns and others. It is a most pleasing picture of life in a country town about 1640 or so, and lets us know how merry worthies our forefathers were, though we generally look on them as being either high-horsed cavaliers or sober Puritans. The honest folk seem to have known little of either the one or the other. Here is Habbie starting in the morning playing "Hey, now the day daws," to waken the good folks; at harvest he goes out with the shearers, and cheers their labours in the field; at kirking of the bride he is there too, and if his pipes do not skirl on the Sabbath day, he is still one of the chief functionaries of the kirk. He is at fairs too, among the steel bonnets and jacks and spears who come to keep order, and "bite their thumb at the Capulets," as we may suppose will happen when so many stout fellows armed to keep the peace gather together.

But soft, now, before we give the poem, we must remember that in Kilbarchan lived "blythe Jamie Barr frae St. Barchan's town," the friend of Tannahill, and composer of the air of "Thou bonnie wood o' Craigie-lea." Here also lived Robert Allan, author of "Haud awa' frae me, Donald," "A lassie cam' to our gate," "There's nae covenant, noo, lassie," &c., also a friend of poor Tannahill's. Here also lived his sister, Mary Allan, who cherished to her dying day some of the poems the bard had given her--unlike another young lady of Paisley, who was fear'd "Rob would write a sang upon her." Allan emigrated to America in 1841, but died there on the 7th of June, eight days after landing in New York. Allan thought his countrymen failed to do justice to his poetical powers; which is quite true. But his case was nothing to the poet Tannahill's. We should suppose that, even in 1810, when Tannahill, baffled by fortune, put rash hands to his own life, our countrymen had begun their course of whimpering over their fathers' ingrate conduct to Burns. But what boots that? It is still a moot problem whether, should another Burns arise, the diners and griever's over their fathers' sins towards Burns would not retire into their shells, and let him fight with fortune as he might. We shall give first Allan's "Queen Mary's Escape from Lochleven Castle," and then the immortal Habbie, spelling and all--

> "Put off, put off and row with speed,
>   For now's the time, and the hour of need!
> To oars, to oars, and trim the bark,
>   Nor Scotland's Queen be a warder's mark!
> Yon light that plays round the castle's moat
>   Is only the warden's random shot!
> Put off, put off, and row with speed,
>   For now is the time, and the hour of need!
> These pond'rous keys shall the kelpies keep,
>   And lodge in their caverns dark and deep;
> Nor shall Lochleven's towers or hall
>   Hold thee, our lovely Lady, in thrall,
> Or be the haunt of traitors, sold,
>   While Scotland has hands and hearts so bold;
> Then steersmen, steersmen, on with speed,
>   For now is the time, and the hour of need!
>
> Hark! the alarm-bell hath rung,
>   And the warder's voice hath treason sung;
> The echoes to the falconet's roar
>   Chime softly to the dashing oar.
> Let town, and hall, and battlements gleam,
>   We steer by the light of the taper's beam;
> For Scotland and Mary, on with speed,
>   Now, now is the time, and the hour of need!"

[Note: the version of the poem underneath is more anglicised than the one printed in the new essay. We considered substituting it but decided to include both versions for Habbie enthusiasts!]

THE LIFE AND DEATH
of
THE PIPER OF KILBARCHAN;
or

The epitaph of Habbie Simson,
Who on his drone bore mony flags;
He made his cheeks as red as crimson,
And babbed when he blew his bags.

Kilbarchan now may say, alas!
For she hath lost her game and grace,
Both Trixie and the Maiden trace:
But what remead?
For no man can supply his place,
Hab Simson's dead.

Now who shall play "The Day it daws?"
Or "Hunt up," when the cock he craws?
Or who can for our Kirk-town cause
Stand us in stead?
On bagpipes now no body blaws,
Sen Habbie's dead.

Or wha will cause our shearers shear?
Wha will bend up the brags of weir,
Bring in the bells, or good play meir,
In time of need?
Hab Simson cou'd, what needs you speir?
But now he's dead.

How kindly to his neighbour's neast,
At Beltane and Saint Barchan's feast
He blew, and then held up his breast
As he were weid;
But now we need not him arrest,
Sen Habbie's dead.

At fairs he play'd before the spearmen,
All gaily graithed in their gear, men,
Steel bonnets, jacks, and swords so clear then,
Like any bead.
Nor wha shall play before such weirmen,
Sen Habbie's dead.

At Clark-plays when he wont to come,
His pipe play'd trimly to the drum,
Like bikes of bees he gart it bum,
And tun'd his reed.
Now all our pipers may sing dumb,
Sen Habbie's dead

.

And at horse races many a day,
Before the black, the brown, the gray,
He gart his pipe, where he did play,
Baith skirl and skreed,
Now all such pastimes quite away,
Sen Habbie's dead.

He counted was a weil'd wight man,
And fiercely at football he ran:
At every game the gree he wan
For pith and speed.
The like of Habbie was na then,
But now he's dead.

And then, besides his valiant acts,

At bridals he wan many placks,
He bobbed ay behind fo'ks backs,
And shook his head,
Now we want many merry cracks,
Sen Habbie's dead.

He was convoyer of the bride,
With Kittock hinging at his side:
About the kirk he thought a pride
The ring to lead.
But now we may gae but a guide,
For Habbie's dead.

So well's he keeped his decorum,
And all the stots of Whipmeg-morum,
He slew a man, and wae's me for him,
And bare the fead!
But yet the man wan hame before him;
And was not dead.

Ay whan he play'd, the lasses leugh,
To see him teethless, auld and teugh,
He wan his pipes beside Borcleugh,
Withouten dread:
Which after wan him gear enough,
But now he's dead.

Ay whan he play'd, the gaitlings gedder'd,
And whan he spake, the carl bledder'd;
On Sabbath days his cap was fedder'd,
A seemly weid.
In the kirk-yeard his mare stood tedder'd,
Where he lies dead.

Alas! for him my heart is sair,

For of his springs I gat a skair,
At every play, race, feast, and fair,
But guile or greed.
We need not look for piping mair,
Sen Habbie's dead.

* * * * *

HABBIE SIMPSON: A NEW ESSAY.
BY
CHRIS MORRISON AND NORMA J. LIVO.

KILBARCHAN, the home of Habbie Simpson, lies in Renfrew district, a few miles south-west of Paisley. It is said that one of the earliest references to the village lies in a charter of 1483 where Robert Craufurd of Auchinnames conceded the lands of Auchinnames, County of Renfrew, along with the patronage of the Chapel of St. Katrine to his son James. However, it takes its name from Saint Barchan, a contemporary of St. Mirin, who lived from around 550-610 A.D. Today, Kilbarchan is still a leafy sleepy place, possessing all the charm of an old world country village.

The village is famous for its hand-loom weaving industry. From the late seventeenth century onwards the number of weavers increased and it expanded into a prosperous weaving community. By the end of the eighteenth century it had a population of about 2,500 Habbies. There were a few hundred hand-looms worked by individual families, three bleach fields, two candle works, a linen factory and a brewery. The names of Barbour, Speirs and Houston are well known to Habbies with regard to these industries. The later nineteenth century saw the decline of this prosperity although Kilbarchan ladies at this time had an excellent reputation as being proficient in embroidery or tambouring of which many samples still exist. Today, weaving in Kilbarchan lives on in history and legend.

Kilbarchan village, with its old weavers' cottages, is full of character and interest and for this reason special parts were designated conservation areas by the District Council sometime ago. A conservation area is defined as "an area of special architectural or historic interest, the character of which it is desirable to preserve or enhance". It is thus no accident that Kilbarchan has a delightful folk museum. This is the Weaver's Cottage in the care of the National Trust for Scotland. A combined workshop and dwelling, it has former weaver Willie Meikle's loom, in full working order, and most of the contents of his shop on the lower floor. The upper floors focus upon a typical weaver's home.

However, it is not the Weaver's Cottage we want to look at in this story, nor is it Glentyan House, probably the finest property in Kilbarchan, but rather the robustly Scottish looking Steeple Hall that literally graces the centre of the village. About 75 feet high; it is believed to have been built around 1755 by master mason, David Kerr, for local landowner James Milliken. He gave it to the Parish Church in 1857. Ownership was transferred to Kilbarchan District Council in 1894 and it currently belongs to Renfrew District Council. Designed as both school and meal-market it proved inadequate and was rebuilt in 1782. It was felt that the school was too small. From its earliest days it had a bell that was rung at six o'clock in the morning, six o'clock in the evening, and ten o'clock at night. It also has an antique clock. One dial face was seated on the north side but three more faces were added in 1782. A balustrade was placed above the clock faces with a number of balusters. Visitors to

Kilbarchan always seem to find themselves swept in front of this Steeple building while they figure out their bearings. It is a landmark. When they feel kind of lost and look up they see a figure that resembles a piper and it makes them wonder about things. It has something to do with the angle of the figure. The steeple has a niche that contains a statue of Habbie Simpson, the legendary piper of Kilbarchan. In 1822, a wooden statue of Habbie Simpson was placed in this niche. This was replaced with a bronze statue in 1932. The original was carved by Archibald Robertson of Greenock and gifted to the Habbies. He took a keen interest in the history of Habbie Simpson after visiting Kilbarchan as a young man. Apparently Robertson was a ship figurehead carver who later moved to Liverpool, another bustling seaport in the early nineteenth century, where he made a fair name for himself as an artist working with wood. He seemed to have been rated as a wood carver. According to T.G. Snoddy in his charming book, *Round About Greenock,* the celebrated artist Chantrey was keen to train Archibald Robertson as a sculptor but the cost involved appeared to have been an issue to the wood carver. Sir Francis Leggatt Chantrey (1781-1841) was one of the best sculptors of his generation. Because of the acuity he possessed for character study, portrait busts appear to have been his speciality.

Was it serendipity that led the woodcarver to be inspired by Habbie? The folklore surrounding the origin of ship figurehead is ancient. Egyptian seafarers of old decorated their vessels with a figurehead. Throughout maritime history the custom continued, especially strong in Naval ships, until around the early twentieth century. The typical images of carved heads in human and animal form, or mythological creatures like mermaids and dragons, clearly had some magical or symbolic meaning to these mariners. One wonders if Archibald Robertson carved similar likenesses of Habbie for his customers, the ship owners and captains of the time. As a folk artist he recognised all that Habbie and old world Kilbarchan symbolised. Legend has it that at the unveiling of the new statue, an old weaver who was present at the ceremony, exclaimed "My, the engineer who made the new statue has pit Habbie's bagpipes on his wrang shou'der again!" Habbie was apparently left-handed and carried his drones on the right shoulder rather than the left. According to Chambers' Gazetteer of 1832 the sculpture was copied from a painting. Cuthbert Lyle, from whom much of the information here is taken, refers to a large oil painting of Habbie of unknown date as being in the hands of one of the Caldwell family in 1881 who purchased it from a Miss Dunlop of Edinburgh. It appears to have been previously gifted to Kilbarchan Parish Council by a Mrs. Caldwell of Paisley. McKenzie, the historian of Kilbarchan writing at the turn of the century, refers to the painting in Caldwell hands as showing the piper decked out with ribbons, flowers and feathers. He states that it at one time belonged to descendants of the Beltrees family in Greenock and that Archibald Robertson probably used it as a model. There is an illustration of Habbie in his book, taken from this painting, which presumably is the same painting that hangs in one of the rooms of the Steeple building at present. It depicts Habbie as a right-handed bagpipe player. There is also a rather garish bust of Habbie in the same room. Lyle also mentions an old hand-coloured print as being extant.

Memorabilia of Habbie is apparent in one of the village
pubs. Outside is a sign showing the piper and inside another
reproduction of him hangs on the wall. Both of them show
him holding a two-droned bagpipe the way a left-handed
player would.

Who was this man Habbie Simpson who was so important to this village? Habbie was the piper of Kilbarchan
between the later 16th and early 17th century. He made a
living from his musical skill as piper combined with his
craft as butcher. As an old piper he is described as "teethless, auld and teuch." He was full of tricks and was a sly
rascal who winked at everyone as they passed by. They say
the corners of his mouth were always lifted in a smile.
Habbie was a Lowland piper. Today when we think of a
piper we tend to think of the great Highland bagpipe as
played at the Tattoo and at Highland Games, although the
Lowland pipes are still in existence. This is a different
bagpipe with three drones, the third one being quite large,
and has a deeper and more powerful sound to that of
Habbie's two-droned bagpipe. It was Habbie's job to play
his pipes, tell jokes and entertain people at weddings, fairs,
races and other celebrations as well as to pour forth death
dirges for funerals. He was paid with cash, kind and from
the glow of his face, maybe also with golden Scotch
whisky. But more likely those crimson cheeks resulted from
blowing the bagpipes passionately. Many legends have
grown up concerning Habbie. In fact, he became such a
well-known character that Kilbarchan people have been
called Habbies ever since.

A poet Robert Sempill of Beltrees (c. 1595-1659) wrote
an elegy to Habbie using the style of gentle banter. The

Sempills were an illustrious family of poets whose ancestral home was Beltrees, Lochwinnoch, Renfrewshire. Robert was the son of Sir James Sempill (1566-1625), a man who had close ties with the court of James VI. James, son of John Sempill--an apparent favourite of Mary Queen of Scots, wrote some satirical verses against the Catholic Church, one of which, *The Packman's Pater Noster,* was first published by his son Robert in 1669. Robert's son Francis Sempill (c. 1616-1682) was also a poet. The poem by Robert Sempill has the distinction of having been taken as the model of poetry used by various eminent 18th century Scottish poets including Allan Ramsay, Robert Fergusson and Robert Burns. In fact, Burns used this poetic form in at least eighty of his works. This form was known as "Standard Habbie." The poem is not a great one but what makes it so valuable to us is that it paints a wonderfully colourful picture of the customs and folklore of a lowland 17th century country village. It is not just an elegy to Habbie personally, but an elegy for all that Habbie symbolised of old world Kilbarchan.

In tone and content it's similar to a poem by Alexander Scott titled "Of May." Scott (c. 1515-83), one of the sweetest of our makars, was a musician as well as a poet and many of his poems have a melodic quality as if he had intended them to be put to music. Scott writes of the joy and beauty of May and of the games and music the folk enjoyed. He then laments on how this colour and richness in the people's lives was extinguished because of the Lords of Congregation (the leaders of the Reformation) and by their suppression of the folk's old world celebrations. Favourite games like Robin Hood and Little John were banned. Old customs were frowned upon as superstitious nonsense.

Because of the similarity between the poems we have reprinted "of may" underneath. The poem is taken from a fine, privately printed, small edition of 1822, edited by the celebrated antiquary and bibliophile, David Laing. He had prepared the collection from a manuscript compiled in the year 1568 by George Bannatyne which Laing refers to as the "*Ballat Buik.*" His notes are printed after the poem and as you can see are critical to understanding many of the awkward words used and allusions made. Often the letters f and v in the text serve as s and u, respectively, as used today. It takes a while for the eye to get acclimatised and can be an irritation to some. However it is worth persevering as it is a beautiful poem which probably attracted the eye of Robert Sempill.

# of may.

May is the moneth maift amene
For thame in Venus feruice bene,
To recreat thair havy hartis:
May cauffis curage frome the fplene,
And every thing in May revartis.   5

In May the pleafant fpray vpfpringis;
In May the mirthfull maveifs fingis;
And now in May to madynis fawis,
With tymmer wechtis to trip in ringis,
And to play vpcoill wt the bawis.   10

In May gois gallandis bringin fymer,

And trymly occupyis thair tymer,
With hunts vp, every morning plaid;
In May gois gentill wemen gymmer,
In gardynis grene their gruis to glaid.   15

In May quhe men zeid everichone,
Wt Robene Hoid and Littill Johne,
To bring in bowis and birkin bobbynis;
Now all fic game is faftlingis gone,
Bot gif it be amangis clovin Robbynis.   20

Abbotis by rewll, and Lorde but reffone,
Sic fenzeoris tymis ourweill this feffone;
Vpoun thair vyce war lang to waik,
Quhais falfatt, fibilnes and treffone,
Hes rung thryis oure this zodiak.   25

In May begynis the golk to gaill;
In May drawis deir to doun and daill;
In May men mellis with famyny
And ladeis meitis thair luvaris leill;
Quhen Phebus is in Gemyny.   30

Butter, new cheis, and beir in May,
Comanis, cokkillis, curdis and quhay,
Lapftaris, lempettis, muffillis in fchellis,
Grene leikis, and all fic me may fay,
Suppofe fum of thame fourly fmellis.   35

In May grit men wtin thair boundis,
Sum halkis the walteris, fum wt houndis
The hairis owt-throw the forreftis cachis,
Syne after thame thair ladeis foundis,
To fent the rynnyng of the rachis.   40

In May frank archeris will affix

In place to meit, fyne marrowis mix,
To fchute at buttis, at bankis & brais;
Sum at the reveris, fum at the prikkis;
Sum laich and to beneth the clais.   45

In May fowld me of amouris go,
To ferf their ladeis, and no mo,
Sen thair releifs in ladeis lyis;
For fum may cum in favouris fo.
To kifs his loif on Buchone wyis.   50

In May gois damofalis and damis
In gardyngis grene to play lyk lamis;.
Sum at the bawis thay brace lyk billeis;
Sum rynis at barlabreikis lyk ramis
Sum round abowt the ftandand pilleis.   55

In May gois madynis, till Lareit,
And hes thair mynzonis on the ftreit,
To horfs thame quhair the gait is ruch:
Sum at Inche-bukling-bray thay meit,
Sum in the middis of Muffilburch.   60

So May and all thir monethis thre,
Are hett and dry in thair degre;
Heirfoir ze wantoun men in zowth,
For helth of body now haif e,
Not oft till mell wt thanklefs mowth.   65

Sen every paftyme is at plefure,
I counfale zow to mell wt mefure,
And namely now, May, June, & Julij,
Delyt noᴛ lang in luvaris lefure,
But welt zour lippis & labor hully.   70

NOTES:--

'The month of flowers' was no less a favourite theme with our early poets, than it has been, since the days of Chaucer with those of England. Scott chiefly alludes in this poem to the May-games, which in general, being well known, require in this place no comment.

9.-- '*Tymmer wechtis,*' i.e. tambour sieves. "In shape, size, and materials, they resemble the upper part of a drum, and are still commonly used in the winnowing of corn. Both the words are more immediately of Belgic origin; wechts from waegen, vacillare, commoveri; tymmer, a variation of tamboer, tympanum."--SIBBALD.-- See also Jamieson sub voc. wecht.

10.-- '*Upcoil with the bawis,*' "to play with handballs, perhaps by throwing up and again kepping or catching them; a diversion which was greatly practised about this season of the year; as were also the games of Robin Hoid, Littil John, and the Abbot of Unreason, mentioned in this poem, for the suppression of which, our poet expresses no small regret; accompanied with a satirical allusion, we may suppose, to the Lords of the Congregation about 1562. Sir Walter Scot of Buck-cleugh, to whom the poet might probably be allied, was one of the Queen's most firm and zealous supporters."--SIBBALD.

Had he said that this poem was written a few years previous to the Reformation, his opinion might have been acquiesced in:--but this would not have afforded him occasion to favour the reader with some of his usual conjectures.

13.-- '*Hunt's vp,*' a popular air or melody of the time. It is mentioned by some of our other early writers. See Ritson's Scotish Songs, (Hist. Essay, p. xcix.).

16 and 17.-- '*In May quhen men.*' From the Act of Parliament, A.D. 1557, which ordained, "that in all tyme cumming na maner of persoun be chosin Robert Hude, nor Lytill Johne, Abbot of Vnreasoun, Quenis of Maij, nor vtherwise, nouther in Burgh, nor to landwart, in ony tyme to cum." (Acts, v. ii. p.500.)--it appears that it was necessary for the government to interfere, and that this prohibition be made at a time when the Court was opposed to the doctrines of the Reformation.

Maitland relates, that, in the year 1561, on the populace Edinburgh being prevented by the Magistrates from making a play called *Robin Hood,* a considerable tumult took place. [History of Edinburgh, p. 31.]

In Knox's history a more minute account will be found of these dis urbances which 'the rascal multitude' occasioned. [edit. Edin. 1731 p. 269.]

21.-- '*Abbots but rule.*' Dr. Jamieson has the following note upon this stanza: "Here, while the poet insinuates that such games had formerly been customary in to beginning of May, he beautifully alludes to the disordered state of Society in his own time; declaring that the season alloted for the games did not suffice for those who really acted the part of Abbots by, i.e. *against* Rule, and Lords *without* Reason; as they greatly *owerweiled,* or exceeded the proper time. There would be a great *waiking* or vacation, did others wait till they had finished their *vyce,* or part in the play. Perhaps, indeed, he uses *vyce* in the same manner in which he used *by,* as capable of a double sense, and signifying that theirs was truly a *vicious* part [Dict. Vol. i.--see also vol. ii. s.v. *Ourweill.*]

The character of the Abbot of Unreason, and the pastimes and mummeries, that served at this period of the year, during the times of Popery, to divert the lower classes of the people, have become familiar to the modern reader by the spirited and faithful descriptions, given in one of his later productions, by the 'author of Waverley.' The curious passage respecting these, in Stubbe's Anatomie of Abuses is well known, and has been often quoted.

32.-- '*Comanis.*' This word in the Manuscript is not very intelligible; it possibly may be 'conannis or cunings,' rabbits.

44.--'*Revers and prikkis.*' "The long and short distances at shooting with the bow and arrow.--SIBBALD.

'The rovers at which the archers shott,' RAMSAY. But at *rovers* E. signifies, without any particular aim. The expression seems therefore to mean, at random, as opposed so shooting at a mark; from French *au revers,* backward, cross.--JAMIESON.

But the best explanation may be given in the words of our amusing historian, Pitscottie, when he alludes to, 'the contention of archerie,' in 1529, at St. Andrew's. "Quhill at the last," (he says,) "the kingis mother favoured the Inglismen, becaus shoe was the king of Inglandis sister: and, thairfoir, shoe tuik ane waigeour of archerie vpoun the Inglischma-nis handis, contrair the king hir Bone, and any half duzoun Scottismen, aither nobilmen, gentilmen, or yeamanes; that so many Inglischmen sould *schott againes thame at riveris, butts, or prick-bonnet.*" [p. 348.] The wager laid was 'ane hundreth crownes, and ane tune of wine pandit on everie syd': it was gained by the 'Scottie archeris,'

56-- *'Till Lareit.'* The Chapel of 'our Lady of Loretto,' situated a little eastward from Mussclburgh about six miles from Edinburgh. Lyndsay says,

> 'I haue sene pas ane marvellous multitude,
> Young men and wemen flingand on thair feit;
> Under the fore of fenzeit sanctitude,
> For till adorne ane image in Lareit.'

Sempill similarly sighs over the passing of the old games and pastimes that Habbie kept alive. In this day of the car, the supermarket, the TV, the night shift and the Internet; of environmental pollution and global warming, there exists an estrangement with the cycle of the seasons. The poem on Habbie brings this all back home, reminding us of those times, like harvest-time for instance, when we danced for joy together, forgetting all social divisions. Since so many of the legends of Habbie are evident in this poem, let us present it here for future reference. The edition of the poem is as printed in Cuthbert Lyle's "Poems and Ballads of Kilbarchan." This takes the introductory epitaph from "The Paisley Repository" (c. 1808) and the poem from "The Harp of Renfrewshire" (1821) edited by William Motherwell.

ELEGY ON HABBIE SIMPSON
THE LIFE AND DEATH
of the
FAMOUS PYPER OF KILBARCHAN
or

The Epitaph of Habby Simpson
Quha on his Drone bore bony Flags;
He maid his cheiks as reid as crimson,
And bobbit quhan he blew his Bags.

Kilbarchan now may be alace!
For scho hes lost hir game and grace,
Bayth Trixie and the Maidin-trace,
Bot quhat remeid!
For na man can supply his place;
Hab Simpson's deid.

Now quha shall play The day it dawis,
Or, Hunt up, quhen the cock he crawis;
Orquha can for owr kirk-townis caus
Stand us in steid?
On bag-pypis now na body blawis,
Sen Habbie's deid.

Or, quha will caus our scheirers scheir;
Quha will bank up the bragis of weir,
Bring in the bellis, or gude play meir,
In time of need?
Hab Simpson coud. Quhat neid ye speir?
Bot now he's deid.

Sae kyndly to his nichtbouris neist,
At Beltane and Sanct Barchan's feast,
He blew, and then hald up his briest
As he war weid;

Bot now we neid na him arreist,
For Habbie's deid.

At fairis he playit befoir the speir-men,
And gaillie graithit in thair geir, quhen
Steill bonetis, jakis, and swordis sa cleir then,
Lyke ony beid;
Now quha shall play befoir sic weir-men
Sen Habbie's deid?

At Clark-playis quhen he wont to cum,
His pype playit trimlie to the drum;
Lyke bykes of beis he gart it bum
An tuneit his reid;
Bot now our pypes may a' sing dum,
Sen Habbie's deid.

And at hors racis mony a day,
Befoir the blak, the brown, and gray,
He gart his pypis quhan he did play,
Bayth skirl and screid;
Now al sic pastymis quyte away,
Sen Habbie's deid.

He countit was ane weild wicht man,
And ferslie at fute-ball he ran:
At everie game the gre he wan
For pith and speid;
The lyke of Habbie was na then;
Bot now heis deid.

And then besyde his valyiant actis,
At bridalis he wan mony plackis;
He bobbit aye behind fowks bakis,
And schuke his heid;
Now we want mony merrie crackis

Sen Habbie's deid.

He was convoyer o' the bryde,
Wi' bittock hingand at his syde;
About the kirk he thocht a pryde
The ring to leid;
Now we maun gae bot ony guyde,
For Habbie's deid.

Sa weill's he keipit his decorum,
And all the stotis of Quhip Meg Morum,
He slew a man, and waes me for him,
And bare the feid;
And yet the man wan hame befoir him,
And wasna deid.

Aye quhen he playit, the lassis leuch
To sie him teethless, auld and teuch;
He wan his pypis beside Bar-cleuch,
Withoutein dreid;
Quhilk efter wan hym gear eneuch,
But now he's deid.

Aye quhan he playit the gaithlings gedderit,
And quhan he spak, the carll bladderit;
On Sabboth-dayis his cape was fedderit,
A seimlie weid;
In the Kirk-yeird his meir stude tedderit,
Quhar he lyis deid.

Alace! for him my heart is sair,
For of his spryngis I got a skair,
At everie play, race, feist and fair,
Bot gyle or greid;
We need not luke for pyping mair
Sen Habbie's deid.

Some of the stanzas demonstrate the importance of the yearly calendar celebrations related to the earth and the seasons since ancient times. The calendar itself can be seen as a continuous circle. Games and dances also show evidence of sacred rings or circles from religions and rituals. In mythology and folklore, ceremonies concerning the earth, water, fire and air are universal.

Habbie worked as a herd boy and he learned to play a rustic flute or shepherd's pipe. He herded at a place called Barr where apparently there was a cleuch or coal-pit. There was a fellow in the town that made bagpipes. Habbie saved all the money he earned from herding until he had enough to buy his very own set of bagpipes. After he got them you could hear him practising off in a distance. He learned how to play and became a good player. Before any event where Habbie would be piping, you could see him hunkering down amid fields of wild flowers picking them to adorn his hat. He also picked small bunches of flowers that he would offer to fair lassies and toothless old men alike. Sometimes he stored these bundles of flowers in his drone pipes.

Horse races were a favourite event at festivals and fairs. Just imagine Habbie walking in front of the winning horse after a race. He would lead the winning horse with its rider with a quick and lively step by playing on his pipes. In nearby Paisley the annual race awarded a silver bell to the winning horse and the procession that followed was called "Bring in the Bellis." These celebrations were filled with colourful banners, flags and people dressed in their best. Paisley was then quite famous for its races and, in fact, it is said that it was one of the first towns in Scotland to stage horse racing. Tradition says that once Habbie was playing on a merry occasion when a mischievous fellow stabbed the windbag of his bagpipe and let out the wind. Habbie, who usually was a twinkle-eyed person, became furious at the injury to his beloved pipes. He grabbed his bittock, or dagger, and struck in fury at the man. Habbie didn't know that the sheath was still on his bittock so no real damage was done but Habbie beat a hasty retreat and remained in hiding for a couple of days at Linwood Moss, sure that he had killed the man. Then, he couldn't stand not knowing what had happened so he retraced his steps and met an old woman he knew. Habbie told her he was afraid to go back home since he had killed the man who had stabbed his precious windbag. The woman eased his mind when she told Habbie that she didn't think he had killed the fellow since she had seen the man go past her house just that very day while she was having a cup of tea.

Football was clearly as popular in 16th. century Kilbarchan as it is today, except then it was known as "fute-ball" rather than "fitba!" Habbie played fiercely and was fast and distinguished himself in every game. But of course if he were around today he would be playing at Love Street, Paisley.

Habbie led couples that were going to be married into the church with his music. At those times Habbie played 'Maidin-trace' which according to John Millar, editor of the Paisley Repository (1808), was a peculiar tune for the ceremony of the bride. It must have been a march. She and her maidens were led by the piper travelling three times around the church in the same direction the sun takes. This symbolised good luck. The Scots word deasil means walking sun wise round an object to bring good fortune.

This word has a Gaelic origin as deas in Gaelic means southern. Note that this tour round the church is referred to as a ring in the poem.

On a more stern note: Habbie played his pipes before the warriors at Kilbarchan events. Poet Sempill expresses some trepidation as to who could replace the piper here. Habbie commanded respect from the fighters or "weir-men" as he played his tunes. Ready to die for honour's sake, no Habbie would dare look at them carelessly for fear of some offence having been taken. Arrayed in their helmets, short coats and boots, with their spears and sharp, clear, sword blades flashing in the sun, they would stand around exchanging stories of war. Habbie was the one man who could survey them levelly without any fear as he played the bagpipes.

In those days, it also was the habit that after dinner, people went to a little green near the Pennel thorn and danced at the ring, as it was known. May was a favourite month for the game known as "Tripping in Rings." The maidens danced with improvised tambourines, round vessels that were used for winnowing corn. It was generally popular for village greens to be used on a Sunday afternoon in these times. Couples would dance together in the open air. It is said that these activities were better attended than the Kirk who took a rather dim view of the piping and dancing. `Trixie," a melody popular in the 16th. century was one tune Habbie played regularly. Another was "The Day It Dawis" which is one of the oldest known Scottish airs. He also played "Hunt Up" which is an old air derived from a tune played and sung by huntsmen at the crack of dawn. According to Lyle, Habbie not only played music, he composed as well. One of his pieces is "Quhip Meg

Morum" The harvest time of the reapers was another example of Habbie's musical repertoire in action. He set the rhythm and pace for their reaping or shearing as it was then called. The dance of the harvest was always danced with particular glee by the reapers of the farm where the harvest was first finished. Those reapers danced on a hill or prominence that made them in full view of all the others. Obviously Habbie was central to these dances of celebration. He led the dancers and kept the working folk in the fields in time with his music. The reapers swung their hooks or scythes to the rhythm of the tune. How many Habbies today know what these old tunes sound like?

Beltane, which was celebrated on May 1st. was referred to as the beginning of the "big sun." This festival goes back to the time of the Druids. Fires were lit with ceremony and there was feasting, drinking and dancing to the new sun. These dances were made around Beltane fires in which people leaped through the flames and smoke for good luck. Imagine Habbie setting the pace for these dances with his pipe music. Connected with Beltane, cakes baked in fire were ceremonially eaten. These were oatmeal cakes on which there were nine raised squares of knobs. Each was dedicated to some particular being that is supposed to preserve their herds. The knobs were broken off the cakes and flung over the shoulder during the ceremony in a similar way that some older folks do with a pinch of salt to this day. Another custom was to drive domesticated animals over the embers for protection from evil influences and safeguard them for the coming year. Again, Habbie must have been present playing his pipes with quick music to drive the animals. During Beltane, crosses of sticks that had been earlier dipped in porridge, were decked with flowers and carried to the celebrations of that day. One custom from Beltane remains with girls washing their faces in the dew at dawn. Surely Habbie followed these parades and dances with his pipes playing. Observances of Beltane have long since all but disappeared and been given up all over Scotland. In Kilbarchan at the time of the Reformation, Beltane, if observed, would have been done so in a rather surreptitious manner, maybe a bit away from the village. However in Peebles, a town that in old times had a piper too, the Beltane festival is still an important annual event. Likewise on Calton Hill, Edinburgh. The pagan celebration of Beltane troubled the powers-at-be in old Kilbarchan. It was frowned upon as being heathenish. According to Cuthbert Lyle, records for that time prove that a good number of Kilbarchan folk had on occasion to appear before the Laird of Craigends, the Civil Magistrate for Kilbarchan area, on charges of taking part in superstitious plays. One of them, William Dougal, was punished for going through a kirk yard with "ane drawn quhinger in his hand" and in the company of "the pypeirs and danceris." In 1561 magistrates prevented a play called Robin Hood being performed in Edinburgh. As a result a considerable disturbance took place. John Knox, of Reformation fame, in his history apparently gives a detailed account of this riot and of "the rascal multitude." Habbie must have played for these kinds of productions too as the poem refers to him piping at "Clark-playis." These were plays written by professional script writers and the actors may have been local or travelling players. Remember Habbie was a contemporary of

William Shakespeare, one of the nimblest writers of all time. Plays were the rage.

Another celebration where Habbie would be present was Sanct Barchan's Feast or Barchan's Day. It was held on the first Tuesday of December. In the present calendar it would be held the first Tuesday following December 13. There is an old, old rhyme:

> Barchan's Day bricht
> The shortest day and the langest nicht.

The Barchan's Day Market was at one time of considerable importance. At this fair it might not be uncommon for one thousand horses to be put up for sale. This market faded away after 1900. Habbie must have been in his element at these markets bringing joy and pleasure to everyone there. Poet Sempill tells us that such was Habbie's passion at the Feast Day that he held his chest up high and blew the bagpipe in such a way that it made him look a bit mad, like a man possessed. Sometimes pipers look like this with their blood pressure up and their faces looking graphically like a map of veins from the effort and concentration of blowing the bag and playing the pipe. The authors have noticed it themselves. It can be a bit scary to behold.

According to Mackenzie, who seems to make no reference to Beltane in his rather dry history, there was a summer fair called Lily's day. This was held annually on the third Tuesday of July. It was a public market with dairy and fruit produce, wool and lint, wooden utensils and horses and cattle for sale. There was a cattle market in the morning and horse racing in the afternoon. A grand, colourful procession of tradesmen and officers trooped through the village with flags flying, drums beating and music playing. Habbie would no doubt be present on this occasion dancing along with his pipes playing. Robert Mackenzie quotes an incident that happened at this fair in 1687 so we know that it was then extant and do take the impression that it existed for sometime before this date. It is said that Lilias Day as it is known today was named after Lilias, daughter of one of the Cuninghame lairds of Craigends. William Cuninghame of Craigends was born in 1646. He was laird of Craigends from 1690-1727. He married twice and his second wife, Christian Colquhoun of Luss, bore him four sons and four daughters. One daughter was called Lilias. His son Alexander, laird of Craigends from 1727-42, who married Anne, daughter of Sir John Houstoun of Houston, also had a daughter called Lilias. Rightly or wrongly, it would seem logical to assume that the first Lilias was named after the summer fair, Lily's Day (apparently sometimes referred to as Lillia's Day), and that by this association the summer fair became known as Lilias Day. Whatever the precise origin, it was popular in the 18th. century. The celebration died out around the end of the 19th. century, was briefly revived in the 1930's and again in 1967. Since then it has been held on the first Saturday of June.

The celebration today is a motley collection of various customs and pageants. The people of Kilbarchan and environs work hard to make it a day to remember. Colourful banners and flags fly everywhere. Arches of flowers lining parts of the streets were popular earlier this century. There is a parade with bands and other walking groups along with floats, including a float for the Queen. Young ladies who are at least 16 years of age on Lilias Day and who either live or work in Kilbarchan or neighbouring Brookfield are invited to attend a dance. At this function, judges interview each of them and then choose Lilias. Lilias plays the part of crowning the Queen. A Town Crier rings a bell to attract the villagers and proclaim the news of the celebration while a jester plays the fool. The Town Crier precedes the parade procession. Participants include Sanct Barchan and his monks along with Druids. There is a pageant depicting Robert the Bruce's daughter who was injured in a fall from her horse. Her injury resulted in death and was followed by a caesarean delivery of her baby son Robert. Another pageant involves the Craufurd Family of the castle of Auchenames as well as Baron William Cunninghame of Craigends and his family. Mary Queen of Scots also features in the celebration There are all kinds of entertainments. The highlight is reached when passing the Steeple building St. Barchan knocks on the door and asks Habbie to join the parade. Habbie comes down while his statue is draped with a flag. Imagine Habbie lifting his bag against his right forearm holding his chanter with his right hand. He would puff into the blowstick until the bag is almost full. Then he would strike the bag with his left hand and start the drones vibrating. When they were going good and strong, he would tuck the bag under his right arm and squeeze it hard against his ribs. He could then hear the sound of the chanter chanting. As he played, he would blow and squeeze, and keep the bag hard at all times. The reeds of his drones and chanter would sound loud and full. As Habbie played, it would be a delight to listen to the dulcet tones of the reeds. But again the piper who plays the role of Habbie today plays on a three-droned Great Highland bagpipe. The day comes to an end for another year when Habbie returns to the steeple at midnight.

Habbie Simpson was buried in the old Kirk yard of Kilbarchan and his tombstone can be seen there marked by the symbol, a cleaver, of the craft of a butcher.

Hab Simpson's deid.

*   *   *   *   *

A STORY OF GREENOCK.

WHEN I was a young man, now, alas! many a year ago, as I am warned by my waning strength and slower steps, I was working as a shipwright at Greenock, and fell into friendship with Johnnie Blair, a worthy honest soul as ever rivetted a bolt. One little failing he had-had man ever less? This small blemish was a rather strong love of John Barleycorn: whiles he took rather more of the nappy than was good either for soul or body. Notwithstanding of this fault, Johnnie had so many tales and stories of the auld warld, that he was indeed a boon companion, and became in a way a crony of mine. Often to his quaint aul'-farrant tales I did seriously incline mine ear. One of these has both a local and general interest, and I shall tell it in his own hameowr leed, as near as I am able:-

Ae bonnie nicht about the end o' August, in the year 1786, I was taking a dauner up the Kilmacolm road. Ye ken it winds alang the face o' the brae yonner. I gaed up by the Aughmoughton Mills, and clamb up to near Knock-an-air, at the tap o' the hillside. Loshie me! when I gat there what a bonny scene lay down aneath! There was the calm Clyde in a' its pride an' glory! Awa' to the wast the sun was near setting ow'r the Cowal hills, and the heavy darkening shadows of the wild and rugged mountains of Argyle were settling on the Gareloch and Loch Long. To the east a sight of as much magnificence greeted the eye. I could mark the

Clyde coming down by Dunglas an' Bowling, the rugged heights o' Dumbuck, an' the Kilpatrick hills, and the huge Rock of Dumbarton, rising as it were from out the Firth's waters, and standing forth the watchman and guardian of the flood. Ye ken that rock is named in auld books. In Bede's works, which my cousin the minister of Knockhardy lent me to read, I see it's cau'd Al-Cluith, which behoves to hae been the Gaelic o' that day for the Stone of the Clyde, a very meet name for't forsooth. Awa' ow'r on the other side o' the water lay Cardross, its winding bays an' heads clear to the e'e, the fields and ferms farrer up, the heathy hill-side farrer up still, an' towerin' ow'r a' the far-away rocky bulk of Ben Lomond. The tide was in. Ships were to be seen dotting the Firth wi' their white sails, hieing on their various errands of usefulness. There were nae steamboats then, but the white canvas o' the sailing ships made a gallant sight-better, I whiles think, than the smoky steamers, for a' their pith an' speed. While I was takin my sairin o' lookin' at the country side, the river, and Greenock down on the water's edge, an' hearkenin' to the whirr o' the moor-fowl, as they settled in a black flock on the fermer's stooks, I sees a braw buxom lass comin' doun the Kilmacolm road. She was a weel'faur'd dame, wi' cheeks like roses. She had on a tartan shawl, an' was carrying some things wi' her. I offered to help her to carry them, which she gladly assented to, for she was tired wi' a lang journey. She had come frae Ayrshire, she said, an' had got a drive to Kilmacolm, and was gaun first to Jamie Macpherson, the shipwright's, wha's wife was her cousin, and syne to Argyle, where her fouk belang'd. I kent Jamie as weel's I ken you, Davie; we were gude cronies and gude neebours.

Twa or three days after this I chanced to forgather wi' Jamie. "Man, John," says he to me, "ye're aye speaking about books an' poets; ye'll come doun by the nicht an' I'll let you see some richt poems." I gaed doun by accordingly, and got a sicht o' the book he spak o'. It was a volume of poems by Robert Burns, printed at Kilmarnock. "It was Mary Campbell, Jean's cousin," Jamie explained, "wha, brought the book wi' her frae Ayr; its just new out, you see. She's awa to Argyle to see her friends, an' she's comin' back in a week or twa to be married. And wha do ye think till?" I said I couldna guess. "Weel, it's juist to the chiel' wha made that book. She said he had been fechtin' wi' the ministers, an' was thinkin' o' gaun awa to the Wast Indies; but she didna care, she was willin' to gang wi' him." Jamie read a lot o' the poems ow'r; and we held at them till twal' o'clock. Jamie said he didna a'thegither like the way the chiel spak o' the kirks, but he thocht "the lassie might help to haud him straught; and he sudna be the man to mak' strife amang sweethearts." He let's see a wee sang the lass had brocht wi' her, beginning:-

> "Will ye gang to the Indies, my Mary,
> An' leave auld Scotland's shore?"

Which Mary had shown as a great secret to his wife; and which was written upon herself. Mary returned across the Firth the week after. It was a cold, rainy, muggy day that she got to cross, and she had gotten a dreadful chill. The fever was then ragin' in Greenock, for ye ken wi' our houses a' huddled thegither, an' the ill water we had then, an' the foul air that hangs about our narrow wynds and closes, we never hardly want fever. Poor Mary, anyway, took it; whether it was the chill she had gotten, or the foul air of Minch Collop Close, or baith thegither, that brocht it on I canna say, but Mary sickened, an' grew worse day by day. Jamie Macpherson's wife nursed her like a sister; a doctor was called in, but naething wad do. Her time was come. Jamie's wife tell'd me a' about it. She lay in a wee room aff the kitchen: there was a chest o' drawers an' a clock in't, three or four stuffed birds, and a picture of a naval battle between the French and British, also two models of ships. There was a wee window, that neither opened up nor down; but the air outside was that foul with vapours that it was maybe better it didna. Nae doubt to her comin' out o' the country, the close air that the dwellers lungs had got used to, wad no be beneficial: man, I whiles think that thae fevers are jist brocht on by the air a' thegither.* Whiles the poor sufferer was a wee raivell'd, whiles she repeated verses out o' the Bible, ane in particular, "Thor shalt not forswear thyself, but shall perform unto the Lord thine oaths;" and aince she cried out, "O for a drink o' caller water!" but it was thocht at that time that water was ill for fevers.

But afore she de'ed, she was quite sensible, an' said to her cousin Jean, "If it had been God's will, I wad hae liked to be Robert Burns' wife; but I ken I'm deein', an' I'm quite willin'." "Dinna speak that way, Mary," said Jean, "or ye'll break my heart: ye'll get better yet, lassie, for a' this."

But she did not get better; and the night following her spirit took its flight from this world of sin and misery: to the great sorrow of all her friends, and as was kent some years after, to that of her admirer, Robert Burns. Ye ken his song, "Highland Mary," was written about her; an' ither sangs o' his, gin I could mind them. She was buried in the New

Cemetery, an' mony a body gangs to see her grave. If it be true that our narrow streets and crowded rooms shorten fouk's lives, and cut aff in the bloom o' youth mony a Highland, an' Irish, an' English Mary, of whom there's naebody sings a sang, I wish some chiel wad write a book about it-an' tell fouk what to do; an' set forth the charms o' a country life--only for the like o' us ye ken, we maun ay be near the water to build the ships.

With other remarks of a like kind honest Johnnie wound up his story of the sorrowful death of Highland Mary.

*A friend of ours insists on it that typhoid fever is caused by the *ammoniation* of the blood--just as tipsiness and delirium tremens are caused by alcohol. He calls it ammoniation, from want of a better name--but there are other gases besides ammonia--all those that arise from putrefying foetal matters. He holds that the fever may be taken in either by the air, or in drink, or food. This fever is different from fever of the cold, of famine, &c. This theory is here first printed.

*   *   *   *   *

Printed in the United Kingdom
by Lightning Source UK Ltd.
102160UKS00001B/106-117